Keepers

BOOKS BY SHOLOM GLOUBERMAN

Keepers: Inside Stories from Total Institutions (first edition, 1990)

My Operation: A Health Insider Becomes a Patient (2011)

Keepers

Workers in Total Institutions

Sholom Glouberman

Rock's Mills Press
Oakville, Ontario
2017

Published by
ROCK'S MILLS PRESS
www.rocksmillspress.com

Library and Archives Cataloguing in Publication (CIP) data is available from
the publisher. Contact us at customer.service@rocksmillspress.com.

To Susan, Misha, Margaux, and Billy

Preface

The short stories in this book are based on experiences that I had some years ago—they are derived from actual meetings with people who worked in total institutions. I visited a cross section of long-stay institutions in many towns and provinces across the country, including everything from maximum security prisons to hospitals for children with severe disabilities. I taped long interviews with about 60 people who worked in them. Although the interviews were carefully transcribed, they were relentlessly edited to try to capture how people were affected by their work in institutional settings. These prisons, nursing homes, and institutions for the severely disabled contained not only the people who lived in them, but also the workers who came there every day. I tried to reveal the character of the workers and the impact of the institutions on their lives by selecting from the situations they described and also by carefully choosing from the words they used. The stories are my constructions based on the tapes. I spent months editing and rewriting them. The genre has recently come into prominence—an amalgam of fact and fiction. In this case, I wanted to shake our understanding of these long-stay environments and the workers in them by creating a more intimate understanding of their work and lives. I think of these stories as a cross between the genres of "reality shows" and fiction—perhaps they might best be described as "friction."

Early readers had a wide range of reactions, from disbelief to fascination. Martin Amis found the character in the first story particularly prickly and uncomfortable in his skin—probably because not a word he is says is true. Other readers were surprised that this supposedly sociological study was in such simple language. Still others found insights that helped them better understand the tensions in all human services organizations, from high schools to hospitals.

Collecting these interviews was a rite of passage into middle age. I felt that it was time to confront the most dreaded aspects of physical and mental decline and death. I began to think that a contemporary journey to the Inferno was through these places. I was afraid that the hell that would ultimately face me would be an institutional one—in a nursing home or a long-stay hospital. Part of me also feared becoming a keeper at least as much as an inmate. Perhaps this was because I was

Preface

tiring of working as a college teacher and I dreaded the idea of doing it for the rest of my working life.

I found it quite easy to arrange the visits. Most institutions welcomed me and allowed me to tape interviews. Once inside, almost everyone I talked to was friendly and forthcoming. Many had never been interviewed before and some claimed that they had never really thought about their work with someone else. Most took a little while to warm up but once started, they had a hard time stopping. Everyone except one psychologist was happy to let me publish the interviews—she was afraid that people would recognize her and not appreciate her frank distaste for the work.

The original edition of *Keepers* was published by the King's Fund in the UK. It was reviewed widely in major newspapers, professional journals and popular book reviews. It was adopted as a course text for several years. Most importantly, it seems to have withstood the test of time. Current readers still gain valuable insight from it. We hope that all people who work in human services will find it useful.

For this expanded edition, I have selected fifteen of about forty stories to represent the different institutional staff members I visited.

I am not entirely naive about institutions; I came to the interviews after having visited many human service organizations and later, I spent a year visiting and interviewing health workers across the UK with my colleague, Henry Mintzberg. In my present position as Philosopher-in-Residence at Baycrest Health Sciences, I still hear from patients and staff about their experiences, and some of this older material still resonates. The interviews themselves have deepened my understanding of organizations and helped me to recognize the importance of different perspectives on the environments in which care is given and support is created. When I wrote these stories, there was not much that presented the perspective of the keepers in long-stay facilities. We still have much to learn from reading them. These days my focus is on the perspective of patients and family caregivers in healthcare. Much like the keepers, their perspective has not been well understood or accepted by the field, but it is becoming more prominent and I am optimistic that patients and families will contribute to improving the healthcare experience of everyone.

I have placed some comments before the text of the interviews to show some of what I observed. I hope that the material is rich enough for others to gain their own insights.

I had lots of help in writing this book, not the least of which was a

Preface

substantial grant from the Canada Council. Some of the people who read and commented on versions of the text include John O'Brian, Sheila Damon, Susan Tannenbaum Glouberman, and Ruth Portner. Other help came from Arlene Berg, Phillip Bobrow, Nochem Glouberman, Valerie Mackenzie, Jennifer Carroll, and students and colleagues at Dawson College.

Sholom Glouberman
Toronto, October 2014

Contents

Peter, Peter, pumpkin eater
Had a wife and couldn't keep her.
Put her in a pumpkin shell
And there he kept her very well.

Introduction

Nursing homes, prisons, long-stay hospitals and similar institutions have been called "total" institutions, their inhabitants have been called "inmates," and the workers may be called "keepers." This book is a collection of interviews with "keepers" who guide us through the institutions, familiarize us with everyday life in them and explain their work. They also speak about their feelings toward the inmates and their relationships with them.

Most anecdotal accounts of institutions are from the point of view of inmates, such as prisoners, patients, and other residents. Otherwise, accounts are from researchers or reformers. When staff members are discussed, negative feelings about the institutions are usually carried over to the people who work in them. Like their charges, keepers are often stigmatized. Total institutions are our modern dungeons and the people who work in them are seen as dungeon keepers. Their jobs are undesirable and carry a fear and shame associated with institutions. The keepers themselves are often identified with the difficulties of institutional life. In movies and books, the prison officer or psychiatric nurse is often seen as the personification of the evils of the institution: Nurse Ratched in *One Flew over the Cuckoo's Nest* is one of the most unmitigated villains in contemporary literature.

In organizational literature, the place of keepers is largely ignored. Erving Goffman in *Asylums*, for example, seems to think of them primarily as agents of a rather monolithic institutional system. It is barely recognised that the institution may have special consequences for their lives just as it does for the lives of the inmates.

Formal studies of these workers identify them as a particularly troubled segment of the work force, with high turnover rates, poor morale and difficulty in maintaining work standards. Many are said to suffer from "burn-out," a syndrome characterized by feelings of exhaustion and ineffectiveness.

In much of this literature keepers are treated in an oddly dehumanized way. We are reminded of school teachers who are thought by their pupils to have no life outside the classroom and the school. They are not really people and cannot have normal human relationships. They do not have the normal range of human emotions. Most especially they

1

lack sympathy. These workers come to personify our strong negative feelings about the institutions: only someone less than human could work in such places. But just as teachers are people, so are keepers. Once their essential humanity is recognized, they can help us learn about their peculiar role in institutions, and more about the institutions themselves.

Keepers exercise control over the lives of others. Teachers, physicians, social workers and others are also "keepers" of some aspects of the lives of their clientele. The descriptions of work in institutions can reveal much about these other kinds of work, as well as the great array of relationships between those in authority and the people upon whom that authority is exerted.

Total institutions themselves often don't work well. They are examples of poorly functioning organizations which are supposed to provide human services. Scandals are frequent, and most have been targets of reform and change almost from their very beginnings. Attempts to improve them have largely failed. The ways in which they fail can teach us more about other organizations that don't work well—places where the "system" somehow works against avowed goals. There is little doubt that "systems" and how they are organized affect those who work in them for well or ill. Recognizing symptoms of dysfunction through effects on workers can help us to understand what is wrong and may also help to improve other human service organizations.

Philosophers use extreme examples to clarify otherwise difficult aspects of an idea. The extreme environments in most total institutions may illuminate aspects of organizations that are meant to care for people. Inmates are people who are deprived of their liberty, incapacitated in one way or another and are completely dependent on others for almost every daily need. Our interest in them is partly because we might learn something from the extreme conditions of their daily life. Keepers are constantly exposed to such extreme circumstances of the human condition. They are regularly confronted with the incapacity of the aged, people with disabilities, or the chronically ill, and with madness, violence, and death. Their reactions deepen our appreciation of the limits and capacity of human beings.

The testimony of the keepers gives a new perspective to universal issues about human beings and human relations. They consider topics which we may think about but rarely articulate: the autonomy of those we serve, the kindnesses we demand and give, the effects of dependence on human relationships, the ineffectiveness we sometimes feel in our work and in our lives. Such issues arise frequently and often passionately in these conversations. They are made even more poignant by the juxtaposition of the keepers' lives with the lives of those they serve.

Keepers, for the most part, share our strong negative feelings about institutions. At best, they see them as necessary evils—places to avoid at all cost, but which might be required for those who cannot be kept in society at large. A worker in a long-stay care hospital who is responsible for keeping the long waiting list says,

> If I saw that I was becoming senile I would probably kill my-self before I would come into an institution. . . . But you can never tell: I have a friend who has multiple sclerosis and years ago, when she discussed things like this she said she too would kill herself, and here she is.

She thinks that institutionalization is largely unnecessary.

> There are [a] few patients who couldn't survive outside the in-stitution. The way things are today, they couldn't. But none of these people needs 24 hour a day nursing care except for a few who are bedridden or in danger and being fed intravenously or whatever. I still think it's better for them being at home with family around, familiar surroundings.

The work of keepers places them in an environment far from that of normal home life, yet for most of them it is a part of the job to provide inmates with at least some aspects of a home. They prepare and serve food, help people dress, or supervise their washing. In many institutions these functions are so complete that they are father and mother to their clients. In homes for children with developmental issues, child care workers at times "adopt" particular patients as "sons" or "daughters." Parent-like irritation is also expressed. A nursing assistant complains about the lack of appreciation shown by patients in the long-stay ward of a psychiatric hospital:

> They don't have to cook or do the wash or even make their beds, we do it all for them. We work hard all day and there they sit, and smoke cigarettes and drink coffee and whine. They live in a hotel, and nothing is ever right for them.

The absence of privacy in most institutions exposes the keepers to the most intimate aspects of their clients' lives. If the institution contains especially difficult patients, very often keepers will be required to feed and dress them. A crusty nurse in a geriatric hospital speaks with some pride of a semi-comatose old woman who still has particular food preferences: "You have to be very careful of the temperature of her food, when you put it in the tube too hot or too cold she'll let you know, she's very demanding."

Even greater extremes of intimacy occur in nursing homes where part of the daily routine is the washing of patients' genitals.

Keepers are witness to major transitions in peoples' lives. The very admission to a total institution is a significant life event both for the inmate and for those close to him. A common view about nursing homes is expressed:

> It's not the patients I mind so much, but the relatives. They really can give us a hard time. I think it's because they feel so guilty, they want to be sure that we are not abusing their mother whom they have abandoned. Usually the patient adapts quite well. It's a relief for them to stop burdening their children. I tell the relatives that it would be better if they didn't come for a while, in order to allow the patient to settle in. But really I don't want them around because they make such a fuss and cause unnecessary problems.

At times, keepers watch over the gradual deterioration of patients whom they have served for many years.

> I know a lady here, when she came in she was a doll. You could sit with her, talk with her. She would be laughing, joking and talking, and as her disease progressed, she went blind and now when you touch her to wash her, she will start screaming and yelling and scratching everybody. She became like an animal really. This happened over a period of four to five years. She wouldn't eat with a spoon—she would lick her hands. She ate like an animal and it didn't matter how hard we tried to get her to eat with a spoon, she just became an animal.

The keeper's role can have something to teach us about the limits of humanity and of relationships between human beings. Comatose, brain damaged children are still human. A psychiatric nurse in a home for children with severe learning disabilities describes one:

4

Freddie had been in a coma for fourteen years. But even he had a personality. The way he came across to me, he used to make me angry and a couple of other people felt that too. There was something demanding about him. It made some of us angry, and it also made others like him very much. I have to tell you that he lay there with his eyes shut with a tube down into his stomach, with mild contractures. He was turned from side to side every two hours to prevent bed sores. But there was something, how can I describe it? There was something that emanated from him.

At first it seems impossible for there to be genuine human relationships between keepers and inmates—between those who are absolute providers and those who are entirely dependent. The form of such relationships must be affected by the tremendous disparities of power that the two have. Yet, despite this imbalance in power in favour of the keepers, inmates have time to observe and get to know their keepers. There are many stories of how they learn to manipulate their environment, and how they get the keepers to do what they want. There are also stories which illustrate the restrictions which extreme dependency place on human contact. And finally, there are stories which show how really imponderable human affection can be:

I have an auxiliary who is very business-like: work has to get done and she is not very tolerant of patients who give her trouble. She is short, stocky and walks like a little soldier. She has to turn them over, wash them. For the first time in many years, I have seen her adopt one old lady. She happened to put a blanket on her and the patient took the blanket and threw it on the floor and started yelling for the police and government. Her comment was, "One devil left and another one has taken her place." But she has adopted this new devil and likes her very much. It's the first time I have seen her give extra desserts and when she quarrels, she laughs with her and she finds this patient so amusing. It's the first time I've seen it. Well, they are the best of friends and this old lady, it doesn't matter what she does, she can do anything wrong, it's okay with her.

SENIOR GUARD
Maximum Security Prison

Comments

He is a man of about 30 and is a bit older than most of the guards, yet quite a bit younger than the other senior officers. He wears a neatly trimmed beard and well-cared-for uniform. There is a gold rifle tie tack on his tie. As he speaks, he often gestures and smiles in order to reassure me of some point, and he punctuates his conversation by tapping on the table. He also acts out some of the things he says. When he talks of shutting the door behind him as he leaves work, he not only shuts it—he locks it and throws away the key.

One of the problems with interviews and questionnaires is that it is hard to decide when reported data is valid and when it isn't. Here, most of what the interviewee says is probably not true yet there is much that can be learned from it.

Some of us behave in a special way when we meet new people. We make something more of our lives. We exaggerate what we do and how we do it. We brag about our prowess and tell tall tales about our achievements. If it is clear that we may never meet again, we even lie.

Here is a man who does lie. I began to get this feeling about him when he said he enjoyed shift work. But what he says can also reveal much about his work if we take it that he speaks in code.

The code is quite easy to break. You review what he says and take it that his real feelings are almost always diametrically opposed to what he says. My guess is that the results are then not far wrong. So when he says that his work is interesting and varied, you know that he means that he cannot abide the boredom and routine. When he claims that each work posting is different, he means that they are all alike. Similarly he really hates to come to work in the morning; he does as little as he can and rather than calm things down, he most likely stirs things up if only to create a bit of excitement in the day. No one else thinks he's all right and he is never fair.

With that as a beginning you can really enjoy what he has to say, and understand it much better. When he speaks of the others (everyone but him), he is really talking about himself. I can well imagine how he got his job and how he gets along with his fellow workers and the inmates.

Then again, it is not so easy to lie consistently. So he also directly says some wonderful things, e.g. "I'm not someone who says yes to inmates for no good reason."

Sometimes even he has a hard time distinguishing truth from fancy. He speaks of his previous failures: he had worked at many things before coming to prison; he even had his own business. Still, he ended up in here. "In general I'm satisfied to be here. I used to work: I worked for myself, I worked for others." The implication is, of course, that because he *used* to work, he no longer does. Work as a warder in a prison is not (honest) labour.

He tells no one where he works because he is ashamed. "Now I don't talk about my work outside this place to anyone. It's not that I'm ashamed of what I do. On the contrary, I respect my uniform and I'm proud to wear it, but outside I tell people that I'm a civil servant."

His behaviour is reminiscent of stereotypical inmates who never have any qualms about lying, spend a lot of time denying their crimes, refuse to see how they have failed and speak in code.

I wonder how much this man's behaviour is affected by the institution. Is it his way of getting along that attracts him to this kind of work? Because he is like the inmates in many ways, he may find comfort from his past failures in his present work.

Does the system he works in force him into this kind of lying? Is he like policemen who have some trouble describing in court the violence they and their colleagues sometimes inflict on offenders?

And finally, he cannot resist admitting the smoke screen in his usual veiled way. "One last thing: I want you to know that some people when they talk to visitors, bullshit them a lot. I want you to know that I was speaking sincerely and that I told you the truth. It's not often that I talk about this stuff to outsiders."

I wonder how this piece of data is to be weighed. He has revealed a lot. None of it is straightforward—it would not come to us through a questionnaire. He is deceiving himself as well as me. But there are many indications about where the truth lies. And the interview allows us to find our way to at least some of it.

Interview

My work is quite varied. It's never routine, I have to be able to assume any work posting at the institution. I'm happy to come to work in the morning. I try to do my work as well as I can. I sometimes have to settle problems between the guards, or between guards and inmates. I think that the guards and even some of the inmates think that I'm all right. I try to be fair.

I enjoy shift work. Being married, it makes no difference to me if I work on Saturdays and have a day off in the middle of the week. You're not too lucky to be interviewing someone who likes it. In 75% of the cases, the people here don't like the work. There are many just waiting for another job. Or they're here because they can't find work on the outside. It's the "bloody institution" or the "stinking prison." Me, I intend to make this my career.

I have been here for four years and I've been promoted to Senior Guard. It can take a long time. There are guards who've been here for ten or fifteen years and haven't been promoted. Four years is relatively quick; it depends on how you do your work, also on how mature you are. You have to be able to deal with people and to be able to take charge of the men who are in your command.

I have daily contact with the inmates because regardless of the job I do, it directly involves them. Even if I leave the institution in the course of a day's work, it usually involves escorting inmates to the hospital or something like that. I don't have any trouble with them. There are warders who have trouble, but I feel that if I do my job the way it's supposed to be done, I won't get into hot water.

You have to know how the system works and you need some idea of the directives and procedures, the things to do in case of emergency. It's true that it's not every day that these things happen, but you've got to know what to do when such and such happens. If nothing happens, then well and good. But if something does come up, and you don't know what to do, then you're the one on the line. The work is delegated to us. The bosses say, "You operate like this and like that," and you have to be sure that you always do it in the very same way. Even so, it's never the same situation and you have to adapt the procedures to the circumstances.

As a supervisor, I'm obliged to get along well with the other guards because every man has his own way of working. You can't simply order him about: "Do this . . . do that." Everyone is on the same footing with me, and it works well, very well. At the beginning, when I was promoted there were conflicts between some of the men and me, but that was early on, and it's been resolved.

As for the inmates, I'm not someone who says yes to inmates for no good reason. I'm capable of saying no to an inmate and I'm capable of confronting him. Experience teaches me their approach. Even if they try to act smart and they don't play the game, I try to remain diplomatic despite everything. But they do try to get at you. It doesn't bother me because when I leave this place after work, it's over, over, over. I put it out of my mind. At the beginning it was very hard; I used to talk about it with my wife.

Now I don't talk about my work outside this place to anyone. It's not that I'm ashamed of what I do. On the contrary, I respect my uniform and I'm proud to wear it, but outside I tell people that I'm a civil servant. If they want to know more, then it really depends on the kind of person they are and then I might say a bit more. People on the outside think that there are all kinds of injustices here. They have a completely different perspective on the institution from those of us who work inside. You try to answer people's questions about the inside for about a year or so and then after that you just say enough, finished, because you are usually misunderstood.

Work in this place also affects your social life in other ways. I don't let it affect my social life that I work here. But it makes some guys crack up. A lot of that is the shift work. But a lot of them also spend lots of time thinking about the work and talking about it. I don't think that it's a good idea to be inside this place 24 hours a day. It's no good. My idea is that when you leave this place you have to shut the door behind you. When you get home, you stay there. And when you come back here in the morning, you do the same thing. As for me I feel good, very good.

This is a world that's completely apart. This is not like some factory, so what happens here stays here. In fact, we don't produce anything here. I've worked at lots of productive jobs in my life and seen many forms of work. For sure, you don't have to do much here if you don't want to. Lots of people lean back and put their feet up on the desk, and go to sleep forever. It's true that there is nothing here—there isn't any product. Because when an inmate gets out, he comes back in 75% of the cases. In my work, the contact with the inmates gives us things to do;

we have the rules to respect and we have to make the inmates respect them also. Things in here can sometimes become quite difficult. Inmates sometimes become fed up with this place, but there's not much that I can do about it; I can't put them outside. It's my job to make sure that they're here for twenty-four hours a day. That's my work.

Because I'm a senior guard I have some control over the work of the other warders. If you see that he's working with you as he's supposed to, then everything is fine. There are lots of guards here who are too superior. You have to be able to communicate with the people you work with. Outside, I was an employer so I know how it works. I also saw how many bosses operate. My job involves something like employer-employee relations.

Inmates are here because they're anti-social. It's their choice to do the things that bring them here. They are then rejected by society and sent to this place. In a way they are our product. At first when inmates come in, they are given the chance to receive training in some trade or other. The 25% that don't come back, well they sometimes learn a trade. For many of them, it is quite difficult to find work outside. Personally, if I had to do time, I would never come back a second time. Also they don't have a very good family influence usually, though it's really not my place to be mentioning this.

Our work is related to that of the classification guards, even though we and the classification guards have different jobs. Our job is to control the movements of the inmates; their job is to help the inmates. As much as possible, I try to do the same thing. But there is no denying that there are conflicts between us. They're family fights, though. At times we send an inmate to be punished and the classification officer lets him off. I understand that the classification officers have a different perspective on these things, but we're with the inmates all day, and they're not. Sometimes the inmates give us a really hard time; they talk back and call us names and so on. Maybe that's why some of the guards become quite fed up with their work in a couple of years.

There are a lot of bad effects from the work. You are not dealing with ordinary people. It's true that you're not producing anything but you have a job to do with the inmates. Our production is minding them and controlling them. Apparently in the old days, the work was different. Both the guards who were here then and the older inmates seem to agree. The inmates used to have to check every single movement with the guards. Things are different now. Do you know which things you don't have in here that you had outside? Well, freedom, and maybe women . . . and even women are available sometimes. Apart from that there isn't much that you can't get. A man who wants to do something with his time can, but if you just want to sit back and wait out your sentence you can do that quite easily too. There are all kinds of movies, three meals a day, good recreation, and so on.

They even instituted contact visits several months ago. Before that there was a screen between the inmates and their visitors. Now contact visits give us a lot more work. You really have to search the inmates much more carefully both before and after their visits. But if I put myself in the place of an inmate, then I see how such visits are much better. The way these things seem to go is that more and more is given to the inmates over a period of time and then some incident occurs and the administration lowers the boom and the privileges go back to zero. It seems to be a vicious circle.

I don't know that the system can be changed, but I do know that I thank my lucky stars that my parents were strict with me. Parents who say that their children's behaviour is not so bad end up having their kids do the same thing again. It's important to make sure that your kids tread the straight and narrow. Now I'm not as strict with my kids as my parents were with me. I give them a little slap on the backside when it's necessary and I am fair. My work here doesn't affect my relationship with my children at all. Nor does my life at home have any effect on my work here.

Yet inmates are a lot like children in adult bodies. You might be able to do a lot with them if you could only discipline them properly. But of course we are not allowed to do that. Here the guards don't have the right to discipline. It isn't something that you can do these days. Even society as a whole is more lenient. I don't miss that stuff. It would never do for guards to beat inmates. No, no, not today.

You work with people. It's people you work with. There are ways of working that allow you to do your job, and you learn to use them over a period of time. I find it impossible to explain them. I just know how to get the inmates to do what they have to do; I can't really explain how I do this.

If I find someone who is doing something really bad then my job is to report this behaviour, not to do anything in direct response to it. I try to be as fair as possible in the application of the rules. It takes a certain amount of judgement to act in a fair way. I don't have any problems. No problems at all.

I used to work on the walls. In fact, all the guards here have to often rotate their particular jobs so they get to spend some time in different parts of the institution. I don't mind work on the wall as a break from the daily grind of contact with the inmates. Some of the wall guards can't deal with inmates on a face to face basis. They tend to get quite upset, and they are best off up on the walls all the time.

Most of the guards are now in their twenties. It's harder for the administration because they don't like to work on weekends, and they complain a lot about everything. I'm very satisfied with my work. It goes well, very, very well. As for me, I don't want to move up to the point where I'm incompetent. If you want to move up in the system you don't need to be a theoretician; all you really need is to know the procedures, a few of the rules, and have some common sense. If someone has the potential to succeed, he will.

The prison is not a model of society, it's completely different. Inside it's much more severe. Most people here were rejected by society; they did things that you really don't want to know about. I meet people and don't want to know what they've done because it might have some effect on my behaviour towards them.

I don't do favours for the inmates. I can't give them cigarettes or anything like that. Drugs are brought in at times. There's no denying that. And the only way for them to get in is from the people who come from the outside, whether warders or probation officers or other people. Drugs aren't of any use to the warders, despite what people say. Here they're pretty rare because the controls are quite strict. In some prisons you can get a bottle of cognac if you have the money. I can't agree that it makes the warders' work easier, it causes lots of problems.

In general I'm satisfied to be here. I used to work: I worked for myself, I worked for others. In this job I get to put on a tie to come to work, it's a step up from working in a factory. Here when I go, I shut the door completely behind me. I want to be an ordinary man outside this place. When I come to work, I often feel as if I put on a mask. In order to do my work, I sometimes think that one has to.

One last thing—I want you to know that some warders when they talk to visitors, bullshit them a lot. I want you to know that I was speaking sincerely and that I told you the truth. It's not often that I talk about this stuff to outsiders.

PERSONAL SUPPORT WORKER
Home for Children with Severe Intellectual or Physical Disabilities

Comments

The building had been what used to be called a "fever hospital"—an institution where people with contagious diseases could be isolated. It is now used to house children with both physical and intellectual disabilities. It is in an out-of-the-way, decaying neighbourhood in a large city, and has a very ornate institutional air, with shiny floors and wide high corridors in its public spaces. The entrance area is spacious and contains a magnificent carved wooden stairway in the late Victorian style; one almost expects to see debutantes in ball gowns descending it at any moment. The residential wings lead off this stairway through long, narrow, tubular corridors that can be sealed with airlocks to avoid the spread of communicable diseases. The wards themselves are grim, crowded with children and apparatus and filled with the usual strong institutional smells.

For a long time, the residents were given only custodial care. But new styles of treatment have been introduced and a large number of new workers have come. Still, this remains a place for children who cannot be kept at home. They are said to require institutional care.

When she comes into the interview room, she says teasingly that everyone is afraid to talk to me, and that she has decided to be the brave one who will try it. She is "the life of the party"; by far the best dressed of all the workers in the institution. Her hair is done and she is made up to look as if she works in a city office. Much of what she says is accompanied by smiles or laughter.

Her talk about Maureen, her favourite, has many levels. It is about the systematic difficulties of working in the institution. But it is also about status, normality and prejudice that enter the institutional world.

She always comes back to Maureen. She compares Maureen with her own daughter. She connects prejudice against blacks with prejudice about people with disabilities. She herself values normality (whiteness?)

14

very highly. Maureen, who is white, has a disability. But you wouldn't know it except for the little tumours on her face. Her own child, who is black, is normal.

Her concern for status emerges when she suddenly says, "When I first came here, I don't think there were so many blacks working here but now there are. I don't know if it's because they are living in the neighbourhood or what. Now the majority is black. All the children are white except one black."

This seems to have diminished the status of the hospital in her eyes. But her own status has risen from her beginnings as a rehabilitation worker to her present role as special education teacher. She looks forward to higher qualifications and more responsibility. She takes these responsibilities seriously. She is very proud of her work with Maureen and she sees the work as made much more difficult by the system of care necessary in the institution.

A big part of institutional life is the fact that no worker is there for 24 hours a day, seven days a week. In fact, shift changes are a big part of the day and they result in much of the awkwardness of institutional life. Who bathes the patient? Who dresses them? Who feeds them each meal? Who medicates them, exercises them, takes them out, etc.? In order to share this work, reduce the size of overnight and weekend shifts, and keep the kitchen open for no more than 16 hours, there are many contortions in the daily life of workers and inmates that are for the sake of efficiency or to make sure that everything can be done by limited staff.

Handing over responsibility of patients from shift to shift means passing on the mood of the hour. Sometimes one shift will undo what the previous shift has done. For inmates, it means having as many as six different sets of workers in a week (three shifts on weekdays and three more shifts on weekends). She is concerned about the impact of all this change on the continuity of care for her charges. If she begins to toilet train someone, her work can be undone by care workers on other shifts.

Interview
In this hospital most of our children not only have intellectual disabilities, they also have physical disabilities and some have other mental health issues. There are some who can help themselves and some who

cannot. Right now, I am dealing with one of the regulars. Maureen came into the institution when she was four. She was very hyperactive then. She would have feces in her bed and she would sit and play with it, and she had to be restrained most of the time. Since those last years I have been working with her, not on a daily basis. I have worked with her for 12 years. Now she can wash, dress and is independent in most of her ways. She flushes the toilet; she is on a dish washing program where she has to be supervised most of the time.

I really feel pleased about her because of the way she was before and how she has improved over the years. It makes me feel good. She was only given a period of time to live and she has been here 14 years. She is seventeen now. I have worked here for 12 years so I have seen her since I came. She is my favourite. I work with her almost every day. I consider her like a relative—like my daughter. I think she looks forward to being with me although she is close with her mother. The one she probably listens to the most is me. If I am not there, she takes advantage of the situation, which I don't let her get away with.

She is here now but she is going to a camp next week. I would have gone with her, but I can't get a babysitter for the night. I also have a child who is 8 years old. So it is as if I have two children because most of the time, the staff says, "Here is your little girl." Once she was sick and went to hospital, and they called me at home and told me so I would be able to see her on my own time (I was on holidays). So I laughed and I went.

My own daughter is eight years old now. I started working here before and I was also pregnant when I was working here. Oh yes, she is very together. Most things she does for herself and sometimes she will want to cook an egg for herself; sometimes I let her do it because she knows about cookers. And sometimes my back will hurt and she will come and rub it. I guess she was like me growing up. My mother told me that.

The shift work doesn't really affect my family. Right now my daughter is in daycare so there is no problem and when she comes home she goes to my mother. If I have to work to 1:00 in the morning, there is always someone there and most of my family are here so I have no problem with getting someone to look after her. When she is at school I have a cousin who she goes home with. And sometimes I'm off for the weekend and we go camping.

My daughter always says, "When I grow up I'm going to be a nurse just like you." And I would like her to do whatever she decides. Sometimes she tells me what to do. Like I used to take the Pill and it's so funny because sometimes she comes up to me and says, "Mummy, don't forget to take the Pill," and she comes with a glass of water and she hands one to me and says, "Let's see which one—Tuesday or Wednesday." But I don't hide nothing from her. Like one day she saw my sister's stomach when it was big so she said "Mummy, what's wrong? So I said "She's pregnant." So she said to her, "You have a baby in there." And to me, "When you were pregnant I was there too?" So I said, "You was in me."

Working here helps me to raise my child. It helped me to see a lot and really to be thankful because if I had a child like Maureen . . . it's really something to cherish. She can walk. She's no problem. I can take Maureen any place, any restaurant. She eats like a normal person. The only thing with Maureen is that she can't talk, but she eats with a knife and fork. If you see her eating out, you wouldn't think that she has these disabilities. But you might think it because of her disease that gives her little tumours.

When I first came here, I don't think there were so many blacks working here but now there are. I don't know if it's because they are living in the neighbourhood or what. Now the majority is black. All the children are white except one black.

My husband also works at a hospital but it is a general hospital. He says he doesn't know how I can work with children like that. When I took some of them to my house they couldn't get over the fact that children like that exist.

Another thing too, I find that you get so much criticism from the people in public. For example, yesterday we went to a pool and a man said, "You see all of these kids—they should be killed." One of the residents was crippled and in a wheelchair, so this man thought he didn't have any purpose in life and I feel that is wrong. I think in order to do anything, you have to teach the community first of all because anytime you go with them, you see all the eyes staring at you. I don't know why they stare. But I know that most people find people with disabilities hard to take. But when I first saw them, I felt a kind of pity because I had never seen anything like them before. I would think I was going to hurt them but when 1 got used to them, they are the same people just like me or you and they have the same rights.

They have the same rights, the same feelings. It's the same thing. Like sex. For example, there is some truth that they masturbate. Someone will come around and see them and say, "You are a bad boy—stop that." He's not a bad boy—it's just natural. You just leave them alone. In fact, the person is usually in a private area and you can't see them. Some people can't accept that—they think it is dirty. 1 don't. 1 think it is just normal to do it.

This work is just fun. It's a very nice and funny work. The children are very funny. They make you feel like working. They do. They always say, "When you are off the ward, it is always dead." Because 1 always lighten up the ward you know. 1 tease them sometimes. 1 find it very easy to work here. If you was to see them. It's just the way they tease the other children you know. It really makes you feel like home and then when 1 get home, it's the same.

My girl always asks after a resident here. The first time she saw him, she was shocked. So 1 explained to her that you've got to let him do his thing. "He's a nice boy; he just wants to hold your hand." There was a picnic so 1 took her along. She felt kind of sorry too, but 1 told her "You shouldn't be sorry because that's the way they are." She knows that all he wanted was to kiss her. She is such a soft-hearted person that she probably would have let him. It is a beautiful thing to work with children like these.

You have to be very patient because for example, teaching a child to put his socks on, it might take years to do it. For example, it takes Maureen a half an hour to put one sock on. 1 don't mind because 1 work from 7:30 to 3:30 and she has all the time in the world to do that. Another person will ask, "Why can't she just hurry up and dress, 1 have other better things to do." And will decide to put it on for her—the easiest way out. If you do this, she will think, "Why should 1 put on my socks when 1 have someone else to do it?"

Yes, you have to be very patient. Sometimes, the patience runs out and you just have to leave and go away. You have to. You can't stay because 1 know if there is one child and you know she will do the dirtiest thing just to annoy you. You have to ignore her and go your way. She will stop but the moment she sees you getting upset, to make you mad, she will start carrying on so you just leave her alone and she does this more often with new staff around. When there is new staff, she will just act up.

You need understanding and a lot of communicating. You have to sit down and really listen. Like a boy we have—sometimes he will be saying things, and you don't understand him and you think it is the wrong thing. One day he was asking me about a card but I couldn't understand what he was saying about this card so I said to him, "You better go to your room," but he still keep telling me about the card so I really tried to listen. It was a social insurance card he was telling me about but I had to tell him that he couldn't have it because he needed it for the hospital. He was angry for that period of the day because he couldn't have the card. It takes a long time to understand—sometimes it goes on until the next day. And also you meet a few that are very hard to understand.

Some of the children here regress. They have a few here that goes and comes. It's not so much the lack of staff, but you will find that one person will be doing one thing, and then the next time another person doing something and the child gets confused and doesn't know where to go. That was one of the things I was fighting for and that's why I made sure that when I'm on holidays or vacation or days off, whatever, I always I have a second person who can take over during my absence to make sure that this person is continuous. Any time you don't do that, you can forget it. The patient regresses very quickly. Most of the children are used to a team and any time it starts changing that's bad.

In order to be able to do things, the staff must also be very coopera-tive, and take part in things. For example, with Maureen, certain things are left to do after I go home. I can ask another worker to see that she does it. So that is something that I'm also glad for because if that wasn't happening, I would have to keep starting over and over. For example I can ask them not to put her socks on or her clothes or whatever. But she can do all those things herself now, even bathe. Now if she wants something (she can't talk), she will put her hands up so she can com-municate a little and is starting to do that but it's very hard, you know, for residents who cannot communicate and you don't know exactly what they want. You have to figure it out sometimes for yourself. Some of them will make some kind of sign and then you know but for the ones who really don't, it's a really hard thing. They all have things they want to communicate, even the ones that don't seem to know what they want. There is also a resident who cannot talk but knows what she wants. She will go bring it to you so you know exactly what she wants and she knows how to get it too.

If Maureen was my child, I would keep her at home because I find her not a problem at all but I don't know if her mother could cope. We talked about it. Her mother is a very nervous person so you are going to have to look at all of that. Very nervous she is. I guess she would let her get away with things. You know, she will go to the fridge and probably drink a gallon of juice and she won't stop her. But I wouldn't do that sort of thing. For me, I don't find her hard at all. I find her very easy to cope with. I know sometimes she is very stubborn but even a normal child is sometimes.

And if her mother can't take her, then she will probably have to stay. She will never be able to live independently. Though I think I would suggest a group home if her mother can't take her even though she can't speak. I know one of the things they probably might ask for is speech but I still am against her staying here all her life. You see if she can get the type of job where she can learn to listen or use sign language it would be good, but she can't do that kind of thing. She will probably never be able to use signs but everything that you say to her, she understands. You can tell her, "Bring me your shoes." "Bring me your socks." And she understands all of that. I know she might not be able to cook for herself but all those things take time. I didn't know that she will dress herself, but she did. And we don't know things until we try.

If I had a child like Maureen, I would definitely have to stay home to care for her. I wouldn't institutionalize her. I guess it's for the parents to decide. Maureen came here and in a way, she found me because maybe if I hadn't decided to work with her, she might have regressed instead of progressed. You know when I saw her for the first time I couldn't imagine why this girl had to do all these things. Like she used to do her fingers and used to have a piece of string and used to go around and round. And one day I decided that this girl loves to eat and if she loves to eat, then she will have to do things on her own so I started making her dress herself and I used to use little candies, you know Smarties. If she does something, she gets candies. Any effort she makes she gets a candy and it went on day after day. It takes me a year before I really start getting things organized and then she started bit by bit. She would put the left shoe on right and the socks all kind of wavy but finally she got the idea, and with my help and her help we reached our goal.

When I first came, this hospital wasn't part of the Children's Hospital, it was run by Social Services and at that time you were loaded with six or seven kids. You know with seven kids per staff, you don't have much time to spend with one kid. And they didn't have any programs then. But with this particular child, you know they used to have her restrained and tied into bed because she was the type of child that would run away and even break the restraints. So I said to myself I am going to have to stop that and I started even before any program at all. I did that on my own so finally when the hospital took over then they started the programs. But I started without any program. I didn't even know what a program was.

I figured it out by looking at it. You know they used to have her strapped down and I just couldn't stand it and she would make all these feces in her bed and play with it. I would go and untie her just deliberately but you are not supposed to interfere. The staff would get angry because I do that. Sometimes they would take my pay and wouldn't give me it, even though I was trying to do good. When I do get her, I never used to restrain her. I make sure she goes to that toilet and I stay with her. Probably because I was so stern with her but it brought good.

After things changed here, I was first called a rehab worker but then about three years ago I took special education courses and tried for the job I have now as a teacher. If I wanted to be promoted more I would have to further my studies. I probably will do that during September. That is something I would really like to do. I cannot now make up programs on my own, but if I want to turn something into a program then I can write it up and give it to the unit head, who would talk to the staff about it. She is very nice.

I think that my training gives me some special skills that parents might not have. I don't think that parents really know how to deal with children with disabilities. The fact is that they just do not want to upset them. They will have two normal kids at home and there's something that they don't know. How can child with a learning disability be related to those normal children? The child can become better just by being in an environment with normal children. I don't say that he will function at a high level but at least he will improve, especially if demands are made on him. Often they don't want to upset him. Finally, when the parents see no improvement they will put him here and just go. So we become the parent—both father and mother because their parents don't even see them for Christmas.

I wouldn't put a child of mine with a disability in an institution. Where I come from, it's the same thing—putting away mothers in institutions. You don't see that at home because they all live in one house— they go to 90, to 100 or 101. And you find it here from the time you get 70-year-olds and they can't help themselves. Families dump them which I think is pathetic.

There are people who just have to be in institutions. For example, there's a resident here with psychotic behaviour and he has to be here because sometimes he goes into these outbursts—even on the street, he starts pulling his penis and you have to remove his hand because he pulls the whole thing out. I can see children like those being institutionalized. This boy is on my unit and I see what he does. With him, I cannot see him at home or in a group home. I just can't see it. He really has to stay in an institution.

There are also cases where children have diseases which cause deterioration. All you can do is give them care. You wash them, dress them, feed them, see that they are turned every two hours so they don't get bedsores. That's all you can do. You can't go no further. Some of them are so spastic, you have to exercise their legs and hands. That's the most you can do. These children don't communicate at all. One of them, for example, has fits one after another. Sometimes she will have about 50 in one day. And she is deteriorating. We know when she is in pain. She will scream out. We know if she is comfortable or sleeping or wide awake. We always find her wet when we turn her. We can't even tell if she is hungry—she is tube fed.

There is one particular boy here who is also like her but he lets you know when he is wet, he cries—also when he is hungry. With each child, it is sort of different. You wouldn't believe it. They all have different symptoms, different behaviour. Sometimes you think that people in institutions are crazy but you would be surprised to see how many you meet outside. We go to the pool—you know what the man says, "You should kill all those kids!" As if we have the right to do such a thing! I think for him if he had a child like that, he would do it.

For a child who is deteriorating and dying, all we can do is wait for his time. When it comes, there is nothing more you can do—nothing at all. We can see to all the necessary things—that he is comfortable, that he eats well, give him his check-up—dental, ECG, everything to make sure that he is not in contact with anything. There's nothing more you can do after that. I've seen it so much every day that it doesn't bother me. There was this little child who used to turn blue sometimes and it used to make me so scared. One day I was watching the nurse putting the tube in his nose so that he could get oxygen and I watched her several times and it came to me like magic. I saw that one day I would do the same thing. But there are a few here who will die. You know when a resident is deteriorating. You know, you can see, so when it comes down to the nitty-gritty, it doesn't make you that upset. You feel bad but there's nothing you can do.

These are things that make your life full. Even if I had to leave from here and go elsewhere, I think this would be the only type of work I would do whether here or in the West Indies, whatever. You wouldn't like to do typing. It's good to go at something that involves challenge, you know, and this is always challenging.

PERSONAL SUPPORT WORKER
Long-Stay Hospital

Comments

He is a slight bird-like man with short quick movements. I first see him on my walk through the institution, the only standing figure in the men's day room. This large space is filled with about thirty patients dressed in white pyjamas. They are sitting in invalid chairs. Many sway a little so that they look like fragile reeds waving in a light breeze. He is a mother bird flitting between them, whispering something to one, shouting something to another, and bringing juice to a third.

Later he bustles into the interview room and begins to speak quickly, and with some emotion, about his work. He doesn't have much time to talk because he has only been given a half-hour break to talk to me. He gestures a lot and at times repeats himself several times for emphasis.

In long-stay hospitals, the endless routine and the time spent indoors makes one feel as if time passes in hours, days, months and years that are all alike. There is almost no change in the routine. The institution has its own rhythm and provides its own and separate reality. Those who are in the institution adapt to it. After a while it becomes hard to cope with change. In many total institutions, changes are resisted by staff and patients alike. Both groups have somehow accommodated themselves to the existing routines and prefer them to any change.

This man has a strong sense of this adaptation to the rhythms of the long-stay hospital he works in. He tells a Kafkaesque story about patients who come to live in the hospital.

Everything has to do with learning to accept one's fate. And fate isn't fair. He has accepted and even embraced his fate. So will his patients. One must simply bide one's time and the patients will come around. His stoicism is poetic and chilling.

The days pass, the years pass, the patients have pain and you can help them relieve it. You give them water when they are thirsty, and comfort when they are in pain, you wash them, and care for them.

He does not question how things work in the institution. They are the ways of the world—almost like physical laws. Just as we cannot defy gravity, patients cannot resist the ways of hospital in which they are to die. He has gone beyond despair. He assumes no burden of responsibility for the patients. They are not there because of him or because of the institution, but because that is the way of the world. And they must adapt.

Still he is a dedicated man. He truly cares for the patients. He sees to their every need. He is their devoted companion within the institutional constraints. Their care is his vocation. He accepts this calling fully and hopes that they too will come to see and accept their own fate.

Interview

My work, I like it. You know that you help some people. You learn about people. You understand people better if you work with them. Many people if they worked here would have no inner problems. Sometimes people outside this place have problems for nothing; they fight for a parking spot and other stupid things. If they were working here they would see that life is so short; then they would understand each other better and talk to each other more. But with what is going on now, life is very bad. It's true, most people's lives are very bad. But here we really help some people, at least up until it's finished. We do something good for them. They can't walk. They can't feed themselves. So you really help some people. And you know it. That's good.

For me this is human work, it has a lot to do with life. These people suffer. They suffer a lot. And we are the ones who complain about everything, while they are the ones who suffer. They are happy just to be able to have a coffee for a few minutes. I think this work gives you experience with life, very important experience. If you work in a factory you don't see these things, you see your machine or the cheese that you are making. Here we see humanity. I am married and have a wife and a little girl, and this work gives me a chance to better appreciate life, to reflect on it.

You see these very important people in here: doctors, lawyers, rich people. But something happened, they become sick, and they come here whether they're important or not. It's something to understand, something to know. You may think that you're poor and you have nothing, but it's just not true. You could fall sick tomorrow morning and then it's finished. For them, life is finished. Why are people jealous of each other? They are jealous of the lawyer, the doctor, the rich man. But you can never know what's going to happen tomorrow morning. Money is useful, it gives you a lot, but it doesn't give you pleasure in living. It doesn't give everything. And here you learn that. People who have money have to try hard to live, and it doesn't always come out the way they want.

You know prisoners who get out of jail say, "When I get out of prison, I go to a restaurant and have a cup of coffee, and then I appreciate life. I really appreciate it." I know some people like that. One of them stole something and he went to prison for two years, and when he came out he told me this.

The work here is human but it takes a lot of patience, an awful lot of patience. If you come for the pay, don't come to work here. It is a vocation, to work in this place. It takes patience, it takes devotion. You have to be human and understand that these people are like your father and mother. They are the same. And you have to treat them exactly the same. You have to think at every moment that this is your mother, this is your father. You have to do that every day. You can't decide to be nice tomorrow morning, and be nasty this afternoon, but at every moment you have to give what you can to others, the most possible.

It is very difficult. It is very hard. Especially when they die and you have to wrap someone up and put him in the fridge. It's very hard. I've been doing this work for fifteen years and I'm still not used to that. I keep thinking that it will one day become easier. I do think that it will become easier. It's very hard, terribly hard. You can't do that just for the pay. Everyone works to earn their food, but here it is also a vocation.

Patients can ask for a lot from you. You have to really listen to them. Listen to them, it will do them some good. People sit in a chair here all day, waiting for someone to just come over and talk to them, to wash them, to give them their food. It's hard for them. They are aware of what is happening. They know everything. They have to sit and wait for everything in this hospital. They have to wait for the world to come to them. They are very involved in all that. More involved than me. Look, I come here, I work, and then I go home. Here they are surrounded by the hospital. And they see death, I do too, but they are waiting for it. No one comes in here and later leaves. They come in and they die. It's hard. It's very hard on their morale, it's very hard on their morale.

After some years of working here you feel that too. You say, "My God, what is life after all? Everything you do is hard. You go to school. It's hard. You work. It's hard." Then you see all these people and you think, "I could wake up some fine morning and catch some sickness, some virus." It's a wheel that turns. The years go by, centuries follow centuries, and it's all the same. Everyone will die.

Some people have more to them than others. They develop their talents more. They grow. Others don't. Some have more wealth, they can travel more than you and me, more than ordinary people. In my work you can't do too much because you don't have a big salary. But you can make as much of a life as anyone, as much as a big doctor. He might be able to do a big operation and save someone's life. But even that can be routine. Maybe I am not a professional, and I don't save anyone's life. So people think that what I do must be easy, but it isn't. It's hard. My work is also routine up to a certain point. Every day I do the same things—I wash them, I feed them, and so on. Everything I do is inside this routine. But the patients are all different. They are not the same cases, they don't have the same diseases. It just seems the same, and often it comes back to the same thing.

You remember the patients, especially those that you have to give a lot of care to. I remember patients from ten years ago, who died ten years ago. I had one patient that I cared for twelve years. He died a few months ago, and I went to the funeral. It was the first time I did that. He and his wife were like family. She came here every day—she didn't miss one day, this woman. She was eighty. I'll always remember that. They became like members of my family. I would take them out in my car, take them for drives around the city. He was pretty sick. He had sores all over his body. I did more than extra work for him, I would sometimes even come in on my days off.

I remember those fifteen years, that I've spent working here. I remember when I first came in here I was eighteen years old. I wanted to go into accounting, but when I got into the last year of secondary school, I knew I would have to go to work. My father earned very little and we were twelve kids, so I came in here. The job was not well paid, but it was secure, and it wasn't a factory. As a whole I like working here, but I would have liked to do something else, become an accountant. Most of the people who came to work here in those days left within a year. In one year, a thousand different people passed through here.

There were ones who only stayed for a couple of hours and left. But for the last couple of years it has become stable. There is less work around, and this job is secure, and there is better pay than there used to be.

I think that you can't teach someone to do this work. The kids who come in from the colleges to intern leave after a couple of months and don't come back. I don't think that you can or should become a helper in that way. Look, once you go to college you get a professional degree and you can work anywhere. Why should they work as a helper here? They take their training and go somewhere else.

I would say that this is a good job to have for a summer, to see humanity to get some experience in life, but not forever, not as a life job, at least I wouldn't want my little girl to do it. I do think that if many more young people came here to work for a few months it would do them some good—not to sit and look, but to work. I think there would be less divorce, less personal trouble. If only people would compare their lives to the patients here.

The young patients used to be people who were paralyzed in car accidents. Now more of them are getting younger because of multiple sclerosis. These patients are very difficult. They don't accept their disease; they understand everything and are quite aware of everything, but they are completely disabled. You can talk to them and they can barely talk back, but not because they don't understand. It takes years for them to accept their disease. The social workers have to work with them for a long time to get them to accept their disease. If you're with them here you still have to do your work, and you can't stop. But they want your complete attention and at times you don't have time to talk.

When I talk to the patients, I always speak English. None of my work is in my own language. Sometimes someone speaks a bit of Spanish, but mostly not. When I came here I didn't know a word of English. At that time I travelled a lot and had a chance to learn English. In other places people speak only English, so I learned.

I'm not afraid of planes when I travel. Life is too valuable to be afraid. Life is still good, I can go places once in a while. If the Good Lord lets me live, that's wonderful. When I travel I see the same people everywhere. There are good ones and bad ones. Why does one person get sick and not another? "Why did this happen to me and not someone else?" they ask. No one knows. It's in the hands of God. The supreme being. I'm a religious man. We don't have control. It's not bad people who do evil, they don't always choose to do it themselves—they have a bad childhood or maybe bad friends, or they don't have work or something like that. It's not bad people who get sick.

You do some good for them. The days pass, the years pass, the patients have pain and you can help them relieve it. You give them water when they are thirsty, and comfort when they are in pain, you wash them, and care for them. My God, people who have good lives they don't understand what it's like for them. I give them water. I turn them. I give them an alcohol rub. It makes them feel a bit better, it does them some good. The days pass for them, the days, the years. The years pass, they pass for them and it's like that that they live their lives. Like that. You spend time with them. You make them laugh. You talk about what's happening outside, how bad things are. They are not the only ones who have it bad, there are others too. There is war. They are all sick but you tell them, "You are at least well treated." There are people who are dying of hunger. They're sick but they are very well treated, very well treated up until the very last moment of their lives. Whatever you ask for you get. Here they give everything to the patients. I don't say this because I work here, it's very well known. Here they love all the patients.

If it weren't like that I would have left because I couldn't stand that. There are hospitals with all the equipment. They're well set up, they have everything, but they don't treat the patients well. Here, it's not luxurious, but the patients are well treated. They get all possible care. They get doctor's care four hours a day, nurses 24 hours a day, the helpers 24 hours a day. They get their food—breakfast, a snack, lunch, a snack, supper, a snack. And in between if they want a piece of cheese, or anything they want, a biscuit, they get it. Anything they want, they get. They are turned every two hours, the doctor gives them their prescriptions, their pills, everything. There is nothing medical that they don't get. Before they die, they get everything.

There is no euthanasia here. It wouldn't work here. I don't believe in euthanasia. I don't believe in it, because it would result in trouble. If it started, then families with lots of money would give the doctor a few dollars to arrange everything. Slowly, slowly they would get worse and die. And it would grow more and more widespread. I don't like it. They shouldn't do it. It's not a good thing in my opinion. These people have lived their lives—they worked, they earned money, they paid their taxes—why not let them live out their lives while they are able and let them die in the natural course of things? Why not follow nature? We should let nature run its course.

It's true that it's more natural to die at home outside an institution. Right now we are having that experience with my mother who is 73 years old. My father has been dead for six years. She was staying with one of my brothers, but he couldn't take care of her any more. She was too depressed. "If she goes on like this," he said, "I'm going to kill her." "How can you say that?" I said, "She gave you everything, for your whole life." But he could no longer have her on his shoulders. He decided that she should be sent to an institution, and it was my sister who took her in. If she were here no one would have to look after her for more than 8 hours a day, but he had to take care of her for 24 hours every day. People can be badly treated at home as well as in an institution. For some of them it's better to be in an institution.

Because more people are getting older, there are more of them who have to go to the hospital. There aren't enough hospitals for chronic old people, and the overflow goes into the general hospitals. People there don't really know how to take care of them. It's completely different work in a general hospital than in here. The people who care for them there change all the time, and none of them are prepared for the long haul. They don't accept that the patient is staying for a few years and is going to die. They have a completely different mentality there. I think that it's better to put patients like that in a long-stay hospital than to divide them up among the general hospitals. They are isolated in the hospital. Here they are among other people like them and they see that other people are in the same position. They are all heavy cases, very heavy cases, and the staff is prepared for them. If the going gets tough, then we know how to handle it. We are experienced with it.

I have the same six patients to take care of every day. It used to be eight, and that was much more difficult. The strong union came in here three years ago and the patient load went down from eight to six. That was good. Now that there is a union the discipline of the workers has been relaxed. The young workers don't accept orders like we had to. There are no special union problems here now. When we didn't have this strong union, it wasn't so good, because they could sack people whenever they wanted to. If you got on the wrong side of one of the nurses, you could be sacked. We also work less weekends, only twelve a year. We used to often work eight days straight, right through the weekends. I used to work a lot of overtime because I got married and had to support a family. Now the pay has changed for the better.

Still, there is no advancement in this work: no diploma, no advancement. I am at the same point as someone who walks in through the door. I have been here for fifteen years and I get the same pay as someone who has no experience. I think that I could do the work of some of the professionals but there is no training program for it here. The administration knows all this, but then I'm cheaper and I do the work anyway, so it's not in their interest to do anything about it.

There are lots of single men who are helpers here and they earn a fair living. Some work only for the pay, the nurses have to order them about and tell them each little thing to do. "Do this. Do that!" They know what they are supposed to do. But they won't do it unless they're told. Me, I do it for the patients, the poor old people. There are things that no collective agreement can cover. You can have a light load or a heavy one, and there's no way of saying which. It depends on what your patients can do for themselves.

My six patients now are old. I see the same ones every day, and most of them have been here for a long time. One of them is a former alderman. He was very hard to deal with when he came three years ago. He used to become very angry all the time and have fits of yelling. I started very slowly, I ignored his fits for three years until he started to come around. His wife visits him every day. None of the patients I have now ever leave the institution. Visitors have to come to them. For some, like the alderman, it's every day. For others, once a week. And for most of the rest, it's three or four times a year. I do have one patient who never gets any visitors.

He is a former detective on the city police force, and he was so bad to his family for many years that they completely rejected him. They never come. His wife is dead now. He once said that he wanted to see his daughter and the social worker called. The daughter said no, she wouldn't come: "My father was so bad to us that we don't want to see him anymore." It's hard, eh? He's sick, he's old. They should forget their old quarrels, but they can't. He's 82 years old and he's still their father. Your father and your mother remain your father and mother no matter what. What do you do?

NURSE
Long-Stay Ward
Psychiatric Hospital

Comments

Part of us is afraid that we will be infected by other people's illness. This is true even for health professionals who often keep a wary distance lest they catch the plague that has befallen patients. Even diseases that are not particularly infectious can elicit such fears. The story is often told about people associated with the institution who become its patients—the mightier the better. A nurse in a long-stay hospital boasts about the former chairman of the board who is now her patient.

This woman separates herself from the hospital. She does not really belong there. She comes from an acute care hospital and is trained for better things. She has fallen into this place as a result of a series of unfortunate events. She is already tired of it and will leave as soon as she can.

She is not like the other workers. They are taken over by the institution. They don't really do anything. They are "accustomed to doing the same banal jobs every day. Day in and day out, no interludes, nothing exciting is happening, the same custodial care. . . . Nothing seems to bother them. . . . They are just part of the furniture."

Most important, she is different from the patients. She has her God while they belong to the Devil. She is far too independent while they are so very dependent. She is leaving any minute while they will be here forever.

But the place does have its attractions. It provides a great deal of security; it is relatively free from responsibility. So there is a danger of being drawn in and getting stuck in it. She might easily become like the other people who spend their lives working in the custodial psychiatric context—part of the furniture.

While she says all of this, the story of her aunt emerges and perhaps the fear that too much contact with the hospital and the workers and the patients will drive her mad. Madness, too, has its attractions. The

32

patients she says are also secure and free of responsibility—part of the furniture. The last thing she wants is to be infected by the madness and become a patient.

Interview

I'll be frank with you and tell you what I thought when I first came here. I looked at them and I thought "Oh my goodness, all these people belong to the Devil!" You know, I doubt very much that a mentally deficient person really thinks. They always talk about God, yet do they understand anything about Him? They probably think He has somehow picked them out to do bad things to. That's the first thing I thought when I came in here. And now I still feel that way but I'm more resigned to the fact that it's happened to them. I used to stare at the patients when I first came in. But now I don't think that there's very much that can be done to make their lives better.

Before I came in here, I hadn't had any contact with psychiatric patients at all so I was a bit afraid, actually. I was in Obstetrics on and off for almost five years. I came here to take a holiday from that, but also I hadn't passed a new test at the hospital where I was. They wouldn't give me job security until I did, so I decided to leave. I needed security, so I came here where there was an opening for a permanent position. Realistically speaking, I had nothing else to do but come because I had no other real job. I've since passed that test, and can go where I wish, and perhaps I'll leave here for a general hospital next year. Although I'm also itching to go back to the tropics.

I have an aunt at home who was a nurse in a mental hospital and my last visit to her was very upsetting. I never thought that I would end up working with that kind of patient. But as I keep telling myself, it's an experience. Soon I will have to leave because I think that I have had enough of this experience. It's nice to have a break, it is like having a holiday away from general nursing or Obstetrics. But after two years, I'm becoming quite itchy—I'd like to go back to general nursing. I'm not learning any more in this situation. I don't want to end up here for the rest of my days.

You don't learn here because it's all custodial care, and yet I don't want to go into more active psychiatric treatment because I'm afraid of accidents that could happen. There are more problems involved; the patients are more active, have more accidents. I often think about the physical danger. Patients could become violent for example. If a patient hit me I would be tempted to hit him back, and if I did that I would lose my job. I don't think it really happens very often, but I'm still afraid.

I worked in Geriatrics too for two and a half years in a geriatric hospital and in an outpatient day hospital. I enjoyed it. I used to enjoy sitting and chatting with the old dears, because I knew that they had lived. I mean they lived lives that I may never experience, and I respected them for their age and for the experience that they have had in life. I respect these patients too, but some of them are very unfortunate and they have had no life at all. One patient on our ward, Old Martha, is 64 and she has been here for 40 years, but I'm sure we have some longer than that. This woman is a Long Term Young Adult—that is anyone under 65. We have a few over 65. We have patients who have been involved in here since they were small.

And these patients are not going to change, not much anyway. When they do change it's ever so slowly and very little. There is one who is in his fifties and he can walk a little now. I understand that two years ago he couldn't walk at all. He couldn't feed himself, he couldn't use a spoon. He couldn't use a knife and fork. Now he's doing that. I feel that fifty years ago if there had been better science then maybe he could have been of some use to society, but he has had no life.

They become so dependent. We have one particular patient here who I understand was discharged once before. He found that he couldn't cope outside. He kept breaking glass windows and so forth, to get back in. He is dependent on McAndrews Hospital. He always says that he's of no use to anyone. Yet recently he's said that he wants to leave here again and find an apartment. I think that a lot of the people come in to get a bit of treatment and then they become at home here and find it very hard to leave. And they are happy to be institutionalized, there is one chap who is discharged but he comes here every few years almost as if it's a visit back home.

Perhaps part of it is that the government hasn't allowed enough money to the community to cope with these people. We have a New Start program and since I've been here we have sent out two patients that way. While I was on leave there was one man who was discharged; he came back and was discharged again. There have been successes, but too many of the patients are long term, unfortunately.

Some of our patients are more independent than others. They are capable of doing their own washing, and we have a washer and dryer on the ward. So they do their own washing instead of taking their clothes to the main laundry. Some of them have kitchen privileges. For example, in the evenings they have coffee at eight o'clock and one of the patients is responsible for collecting the money to buy the coffee. Although they do have coffee that we give them, it gives them something to think about. They have to collect a dollar every month or so, and they feel, "That is my coffee, I bought it." It is better than the nurses all the time ordering their coffee for them.

We try to do some things with them, like buy their clothes. The patient goes over with the staff to choose their own clothes, rather than we going and picking what we think is best for them. There is one Greek lady, she is a big girl, and she has to go downtown, and she goes and picks what she wants and I think that that is helping her to be more independent. Even in the context of the institution.

In some ways we do try to systematically reduce their dependence. Right now we have two male patients who we generally used to shave. Recently one of them has started to shave himself and we just finish up whatever is needed. And that is just in three months that they have managed to do this. I think it is a real change.

At the same time, there is a life in the hospital. I've been here for over two years, and in many ways I don't really understand the hospital and how it works. Even though my own work is very easy and quite simple to do, I think that the administration side of it must be very complicated. I just feel that the hospital is very hard to get to know. Everything is arranged here, they have the boutiques, amusements, bingo evenings, dances and so forth. And at the Singles Centre they have a snack bar and a shop where they can buy their clothes. A patient hardly needs to go out at all, for entertainment or shopping, anything at all. They are able to survive in here without lifting a straw. Most of them have grounds privileges and they can go downtown supervised. There are some who work, others just sit around. We do have Occupational Therapy for them, but I think that they spend too much time sitting around the lounge.

I don't think that people like this could ever be completely independent, and on their own. They will have to have some sort of custodial care. I wish we had more sheltered accommodation in the city. In geriatric care, they look after themselves totally. Their cooking, shopping, everything, but there is always someone they can call. The patients here are all on medication, and so they need particular care. If, for example, they go into the community and decide they don't need any medication, then they can become ill again. Many of them really can't manage without someone being there to help. That's why sheltered accommodation would be good for psychiatric patients as well as geriatric.

It is better if they can be kept with their families or have family care. But very few people want to be involved in that kind of care. They don't want "crazy" people as they were called years ago because it is still quite taboo, having someone with a mental problem. If people are going to become accustomed to having someone who is mentally deficient in their community, it will take some time, but I am sure that gradually they will be accepted. The stigma attached to it has gone down a lot already. And that is better for these people, obviously. And if they become acutely ill, then they can come to the hospital for short term.

One reason I want to leave is that I don't want to get too institutionalized by it myself. I don't want to become too accustomed to doing the same banal jobs every day. Day in and day out, no interludes, nothing exciting is happening, the same custodial care. Lots of staff here appear to be institutionalized. Nothing seems to bother them. I've heard people say, "I'm only here for my salary." They are just part of the furniture.

I appreciate my own freedom and independence a great deal. I think that I was far too independent when I was younger. Once I was on a walk with a male friend and I was trying to open a gate and I couldn't. I kept trying and trying. And this chap with me said, "You are far too independent." I've thought about that since. There is only one patient here who exhibits a high degree of anger. I sometimes think that it is from loss of her independence. She acts angry out of frustration when she can't do something.

If you have a violent patient, most often you know when they are going to become violent and paranoid, and you know what steps you can take to do something about it. You can usually calm them down. They are all different, and they have their own individual characteristics. We, as the nurses, have them in here 24 hours a day. We can say to the doctor that he should put two medications together and because we know them better than he does, he listens usually. In that way we can often stop the potential for violence among the patients.

I avoid becoming too friendly with the patients because I heard that one patient who was married became very close to a nurse, and then became very angry because she thought that the nurse was taking her man away. I try to not get too involved with the patients so that they become dependent on me. I do have a favourite patient, I guess—Old Martha. Other than that, no one. They used to have a Mentor system where each staff had one patient that he or she was especially responsible for, but it's been discontinued because there isn't enough staff as it is.

We have a very limited staff so that we're constantly caught between the charge nurse and the doctors. Sometimes I do feel like a baseball. There are many people who are training as nursing assistants, and so there is lots of switching of girls, and some of them can give you a pretty hard time. There is one in particular who always tries to make a mountain out of a molehill. And you can get into trouble if you make mistakes. If, for example, I have omitted to issue a doctor's order, then I'll leave and the person on the next shift is supposed to copy the order and report the fact that I didn't issue it. Often she won't report it and that probably should be called cheating. But it can happen that someone doesn't see an order, or she may have been busy and may not have had the chance to transcribe it into the ward's medication book. If it is not done, then there can be a mistake in the medications, and that's about the only thing that scares me in this ward.

Mostly we have a good relationship with staff and patients. We have a good rapport. Every once in a while we do have a blow up, but staff doesn't hold a grudge either against other staff or patients. Some of the patients get upset if they see anyone else upset. One of the patients is especially like that, so you really can't have tension for very long without upsetting him and then the whole ward. You can't bear grudges in this kind of work, and it's a strain in a way. The monotony is extreme. Other than that, I enjoy the job most times. It's not as demanding as a general hospital. Mostly, it's custodial care. Just helping them to be more aware of hygiene, for example. That's more or less it. The patients are already up in the morning when we come. Then they have their baths, but they tend to forget so you have to remind them to shower, or you say, "Brush your teeth" or "Wash your dentures." It's like babysitting. If they have a dentist's appointment or one with the chiropodist, we have to make sure that they can remember to do what they have to. If they can, they go by themselves or the staff goes with them, or one of the nurses. It tends to be mundane. But we do have our crises here because we have three epileptics who have fits. At the moment, we have two inpatients whom we have kept here rather than send to the Medical Unit because we know that transferring a patient is a little bit of upset to their system generally. We know that change is not good for them. Unless the patient is extremely ill, we keep them here on the ward and that adds a little bit of nursing care.

I have often wondered what would happen to me if I lost my mental faculties. It did happen to my aunt. Every now and then she moves in and is a patient in the hospital that she worked in for many years as a nurse. I think it's very sad. She was a very selfish person, and I feel that if one is open about one's life and one can enjoy life, then one won't become sick. Sitting and thinking and bearing grudges and that sort of thing aren't good for you. When you sit back after you've retired and start to think about how you were mistreated, then you can become mentally unstable. That's what she did. She had retired when this happened. It is ironic.

If that happened to me I could accept institutionalization at least for the short term. I think that if you can't accept it, then you stay for a longer time. I'd rather take a short term period in a hospital and be cured than become a long-stay patient. I feel responsible for myself. I even blame myself for wearing glasses. If I had been more careful when I was younger, then I wouldn't be wearing them now. But I don't really think that anyone here is responsible for their being here. I think that things happened to them. One of the patients is a brilliant musician, and I think he might have been quite good in school, and he's here. And one girl is here because she was born in France and during the war her parents gave her up for adoption because she was Jewish. And then they came back for her when she was twelve or thirteen, and she had been in a Catholic family all that time. I think that's what did it for her. Sometimes we don't really know.

FAMILY LIAISON OFFICER
Long-Stay Hospital

Comments

The unit manager introduced me to her as one of his favourites. She is eager to talk to someone from outside the institution. And from the time she greets me in his office until I set up my tape recorder in her small, windowless basement office, she speaks of her feud with her supervisor. Her talk is very energetic. She is proud of her involvement in this fight and seems to relish it.

She describes her job very clearly: she is the family liaison officer of the hospital. She talks about her role in some detail, but in the past tense. She was in charge of the waiting lists and was the contact point with social workers and families. She would do home visits and assessments and identify urgent cases. If someone could not be brought in, she would arrange for services that would help a family maintain someone at home. She was a gatekeeper to the institution.

This is a very difficult position. People fight to get their relatives admitted to this hospital because it is impossible to keep them at home or because they no longer can be cared for in other institutions. Their strong desire to get someone into the hospital is mixed with fear of the hospital.

As she gets to know the hospital better, she also develops these strong mixed feelings. There is not much merit to bringing the patients into the damaging environment of the hospital. "It's really pathetic—you take all these people and lump them together. They lose their dignity, they lose their autonomy." So she can't win. Relatives besiege her to get people in, and she feels bad for not being able to accommodate them. But even when she can get them in, she is afraid that the hospital will harm them. And so her job is impossible.

In the end, she burns out. Her burn-out seems to have two stages. She begins to find her work depressing and is ready to quit because she is constantly confronted with a lot of pain, discomfort and futility. She sees other ways of dealing with these patients but is "impotent to make any real big changes."

Later, a second phase of burn-out appears. The job becomes comfortable and her attitude changes. As she explains, she now does "what I can. I'm not going to let anyone or anything really pressure me. And I need the money so I will work." She no longer does the administrative part, but instead immerses herself in life with the patients—she identifies with them. Like them, she "ended up here," and her depression goes away when she accepts her fate. She now uses her energy to fight with her supervisor and she spends her time being friendly with the patients. She has stopped doing her work. She says that she was lousy at the administrative part anyway.

Interview

Right now I'm very involved in a fight that I'm having with the social worker here who is my immediate superior. I just can't seem to get along with her, and I'm not the only one. Everybody in the hospital has been in trouble with her. She's just a very difficult lady. I'm sure you don't get that impression at first but she is very indirect, very confusing and full of pressure. I think she is very pressured herself and she puts pressure on people. People are having a hard time with her and have complained to the hospital manager. I made a complaint to my supervisor who doesn't work here and it was passed on to her supervisor. So she is more or less being subtly watched by everybody around here. Very strange woman. She hasn't even worked here a year. She has a reputation of having created problems. She was forced into being an administrator and she has been moved from one section to another inside the social service organization. The two of us are the only ones in this hospital hired through the social service organization. All this is coming out now—the past problems. She is on guard now especially since she has been warned by her supervisor. It's kind of difficult. It makes for very difficult manoeuvring, you know, to work with someone like her who is so obviously burnt out. There have been a lot of formal studies done on burn-out. As a matter of fact, tomorrow I will be going to a seminar on burn-out. That will be the first session I will ever attend on it.

People just come and go.

I was married for 17 years and it didn't work. Then I divorced so I went out into the work field with no experience. I took a two-year training course in family education at the same social services organization. I also worked in schools. I did small groups—taught sex education on a very informal basis. It was in the state schools, mostly elementary, but some secondary schools and some adult groups. So I did that for two years. It was a very iffy, non-dependable kind of job.

During my marriage, I worked at a geriatric hospital as a volunteer and I did volunteer work in the community. I also taught Sunday School. I had these little bits of experience along the way. I had just taken courses in teaching kindergarten. And so I pushed myself. If you have the energy and the know-how, you can sell yourself if you are feeling confident. I mean, when I wrote up my curriculum vitae, I couldn't believe it. It sounded too good, you know. On a day when I am really depressed I look at it. I could never write that today.

I ended up here two years ago. There were a lot of problems to adjust to. I had to adjust to working, so I worked part-time three days a week. I had to adjust to structure, rigid routine, to people who I am not with by choice. I moved out of a pretty secure, comfortable milieu of people that I chose to be with—friends and family, and came here where I had to be in close quarters with people I didn't know, some of whom I may not have liked or gotten along with. So it was a big adjustment for me.

The work itself was exciting. It was challenging for me because I was given a lot of room to make decisions on my own. I don't know if I was given it—I took it. I'm in charge of the waiting lists. We have about 246 applications on that waiting list. I would contact social workers or they would contact me. I would contact families or they would contact me, and whatever problems there were we would share. Or I would just be a good listener to a family member and could be in a position where I could provide services. I would try to locate services all over the city to help someone maintain a family member at home. I would run out into the community—do home visits, write up reports of assessments of the situations, bring my recommendations to the manager or the social worker, saying that I think this is really urgent—I think you should take this person in as quickly as possible. So I had (or took) the authority.

I also am supposed to be in charge of the volunteer department here so that I would try to recruit volunteers, interview them, orient them to the hospital routine, and assign tasks to them. Then I had a lot of involvement with the patients in the hospital. I had a few patients that I was assigned to. Sometimes if there was a picnic that was put on for recreation for the patients, I would help out. It's a very loose kind of atmosphere here so that I am really involved in a lot of things in this three-day-work-week job and it never really gets boring. This is really what I do, basically. Also, when family members come to the hospital to visit, I show them around the hospital.

There are 232 patients in this hospital and the waiting list is about 240. Most of the people waiting are already in other institutions—families keep them there even though we may have a bed for them here; they are not ready to let go of that person. Or else they prefer to maintain them at home. People sometimes put their relatives' names on a list as protection in case a situation gets really bad and then they know they have a place.

Beds become open here only if someone dies or if someone is taken out, perhaps because they are dissatisfied. Once we had an inappropriate admission. This lady was really able to live on her own. She just needed supervision and we let her go the day after she was admitted. Most of the time, someone has to die. I have become very, very hard on the surface as a protection for me. What do I think of it? I think it's pretty gross. The idea that people out there are waiting for beds and the only way they get one is when someone dies. I got to the point where when someone dies, I say oh, good, now I can get so and so in. That's a pretty awful kind of reaction but that's the way I feel. So you can help the next person come and spend God knows how long here.

People spend various amounts of time here. There's a lady who's been here 15 years or more but she's relatively well compared to the rest of the patients. She is mobile, walks around. I'd say she has been more than what I thought—I think maybe 20. She was a Jewish lady living in this community many years ago and she had no relatives and nowhere to go so this is where she came. The criteria for admitting patients were different then. Today she would not have gotten in with the condition she is in. She would have been suitable for a nursing home. So here she is and doing very, very well. There's a man I brought in ten days ago because they suspected abuse at the nursing home and everyone was so relieved. I just got a call on Friday from his social worker to tell me that he died.

Because this is a long-stay hospital, the majority of patients are here for at least a couple of years. Sometimes someone comes in and after they have been here for a while, they develop some terminal illness. But we don't take terminal cases. People here include those who are chronically ill or disabled. There is a lot of brain damage for various reasons. There are a lot of patients who are disoriented by multiple sclerosis or whatever and they can have a combination of physical and mental disability. Most of the patients are over the age of 65—they suffer from strokes, Parkinson's and we have quite a few young multiple sclerosis patients. The oldest patient is about 90, and we have some very young accident victims too—car accidents, motorcycles. The youngest patient we have here is 23 years old. He can understand but his parents have trouble communicating with him. He can make some movements with two fingers and so can make signs for yes and no. But he is sort of comatose. It's really pathetic—you take all these people and lump them together. They lose their dignity, they lose their autonomy.

For a while it was very depressing—not at the beginning but at some point. You know that burn-out thing. I found it very depressing and was ready to quit. I found it depressing because I was constantly confronted with a lot of pain, discomfort and futility—patients dying to whom I was attached, young patients sitting here day after day. You know it is going to be like this for the rest of their lives and I can see alternatives. I don't like what I see many times. I see patients losing their self-respect, their dignity. And fighting for things and losing battles and wanting changes. I could see an ideal type of set up. You see the futility of people dying and it's depressing. There are several reasons. One is that I am impotent—I came in gung ho. I was going to do a lot of stuff and then I realized it was futile because there was very little I could do and I ended up reasoning with myself—what am I really doing here? All I am doing is bringing someone from out there in here. Taking someone around and showing some affection and that's it. I'm really impotent to make any real big changes. I'm a dreamer. I see big changes. It's also for me a reflection of the state of our whole society. That's just me and how I see the world.

Then the depression went away. It's my own state of mind too. It's a whole cycle. It happened around the time I was having this problem with the social worker here and I made a decision for many reasons.

One, l was quitting and l didn't tell anyone formally. And then, two, I'm going to get that lady off my back because I'm a real fighter when it comes to the real crunch. l will take so much shit for so long and that's it. So when l made that decision, l started fighting. l complained. l had a meeting with the supervisor. l got all this energy channelled into something entirely different. l just tested out people here to see who was feeling the same way l was feeling because l was beginning to feel l was a little bit nuts, okay. And sure enough, l was getting support left and right including from the manager so l felt good about that, and l had found a project. l was busy with this project for quite a few weeks, was very upset by it and l came back in and things had changed. There was a report for me and she was really on her guard and things have changed dramatically. l befriended someone here who l didn't speak to for a year so we were supporting one another too.

It suddenly became a super comfortable place to come to every day and my attitudes have changed towards my work. l think I'm at a point where l say that l will do what l can. I'm not going to let anyone or anything really pressure me. And l need the money so l will work. Not that l am sloughing off on anything except maybe the administrative part which l am lousy at anyway but patient relations and stuff like that—l love the patients, that hasn't changed. But as far as letting anything pressure me—maybe because l made the decision that l was quitting and l came to terms with it. Maybe that's why l came back with a different mindset. Also, l wasn't depressed constantly over that period of time. l think l saw myself in a lot of these people too. l used to become very attached to patients and became quite upset when they died. Now l don't let it happen. l haven't closed myself to the patients. l am really warm towards them. l really love some of them—l run over and give them a hug but l think it's part of my own maturation. How long can you go on climbing over everyone that you meet?

If l saw that l was becoming senile l would probably kill myself before l would come into an institution. But who knows. l have a friend who has M.S. and years ago, she discussed things like this and said she would kill herself and here she is. You still have that determination to stay alive. l really don't know. l don't like to think about it. l feel the aging process now. l feel the difference, the concern that l never felt before.

l have a belief anyway—l believe that there is an afterlife. I'm not religious at all but I was very involved at some point in spiritual groups and studying the afterlife and reading an awful lot. I have seen things and I believe people who I know personally who told me they saw a vision. I have seen things myself and felt things and I feel there is a connection between the energy we have and the universe so maybe that makes it easier. I believe that there is an energy in each of us.

I think a lot of things in life are shit. You have got to take one day at a time anyway and play it really well every day. So maybe this is part of it. Maybe I got to the point that if I didn't believe there was an afterlife ... maybe I don't believe it that strongly anyway. I talk in such a bitter way but I think there is a lot of violence, a lot of sickness, a lot of ugliness, man's inhumanity to man. So you die. Maybe it makes me think that you have to live life to its fullest. I think it has enhanced me as a person. I am more sensitive. I have always been sensitive, but I think I am more sensitized.

The people here would be better off outside institutions. But our society is not geared for that and doesn't encourage it so it's very difficult for people out there to be maintaining someone at home because they don't have the support or encouragement. There are some chronically ill patients who are kept at home. There is a lady I know whose husband is at home. He has been assessed as in the lowest grade category, and he is totally bedridden, completely senile. She just has the money to maintain him in the home. She has nursing assistants, etc., and she works. She is considering bringing him here but not yet. I don't think it's just that. I think it's an attitude like years ago kids never moved out of the house until they got married—even if they were thirty. Today, it's an attitude and it catches on. You feel freaky if you are 21 and still living at home, especially if you are a man.

I was discussing this with a social worker who is from India originally and they don't have institutionalized long-stay or even geriatric care at all. When a person has no relatives the neighbours come in and take over or if there are children, they each take the parent for some time. They find it hard and they complain and it's difficult but they have the support. They are encouraged to complain—it's an expected thing and they have the support of people around them but there's no such a thing as a long-stay hospital system.

It would be possible for that to happen here. There are [a] few patients who couldn't survive outside the institution. The way things are today, they couldn't. But none of these people needs 24 hour a day nursing care except for a few who are bedridden or in danger, and being fed intravenously or whatever. If there is money and strong personnel to do lifting and washing, etc., then sure, why not. I have mixed feelings. Maybe if the institutions were run differently. They still get stimulation here which they don't get at home. I still think it's better for them being at home with family around, familiar surroundings. I had a patient who was on a waiting list at home and I saw that he died at home and I was really glad that he did. The wife just couldn't yet let him come in here and we were helping her out. I was glad that he died and didn't have to be subjected to being in an institution. It can be very difficult for most people—adjusting and having to contend with the odd frustrated nurse or auxiliary, afraid to complain because if you complain they are going to take it out on you so it will be harder for you. I don't know if I am just confusing you with my attitude. I'm uncertain but I still feel that institutions aren't all that necessary—I mean, who would like to be institutionalized?

SOCIAL DEVELOPMENT OFFICER
Maximum Security Prison

Comments

No one wants to be a pariah. To be disliked by one's fellow workers makes life very hard, to be completely rejected can make it impossible. We have all felt the dread of going to an inhospitable place—perhaps through school or work. It is at such times when no one says hello. No one invites us for coffee. No one chats. We feel ignored, even invisible. We wonder what we must do to make others like us, to become part of the gang.

She is an intelligent woman, in her early thirties, and has a nervous air about her. She accentuates her words with abrupt movements. She gradually reveals her isolated resignation while maintaining a good-humoured way of talking about her work.

Her struggle to work on equal terms in a male environment provides an extreme version of the experience. Institutional pressures of exclusion are intense. The subtle exclusions of more ordinary work places become more overt in the prison and confrontations pose threats of violence rather than discomfort or embarrassment. Exclusions based on sex can have more dramatic consequences in a prison than in an office. The brutality of the prison environment and the events in her story contrast sharply with the mundane aspects of her job. She organizes social events for the inmates.

It is a hard job to get, hard to keep, and hard to do something with. The security procedures, the resistance of the staff and inmates to innovation, and the limitations on relationships with others all make her work nearly impossible. The use of "security considerations" as a weapon of sexism is mirrored in the rest of institutional life where fears for security mask irrational behaviour and needlessly restrictive rules.

At first, her safety in the prison comes from the inmates who see that she is not on the side of the warders. She finds she can go anywhere without risk. Gradually, she succeeds in taming the warders. And then the inmates become a problem. She discovers that prejudice in the institution is not one-sided. It comes from everyone. The closed-mindedness of the security brigade is mirrored in the closed-mindedness of the inmates who also have their ways. She says, "First of all, you have the mentality of the inmates to contend with and they are not open to new ideas. They are so conformed in that that it is very hard to bring anything different in because they will walk away."

And so she must try to win over the inmates to her way of thinking. Her campaign fails because her fight with a jealous inmate turns the others against her. She is caught between warders and inmates with no real ally.

She overcomes her discouragement to fight yet again for her job. But now her fight has become more difficult. She is even more alone than before. She no longer can count on the inmates. Finally, in frustration, she gives up and begins to pander to them.

"What I am doing right now is making damn sure that I don't fuck up any of their plans. I go out of my way to make sure they get the meeting; I make extra sure they get the passes. I guess I'm sucking up to them to put it bluntly but I have tried everything else and it doesn't work."

She has lost her fight.

In the end, she still recognizes the comedy in the situation by telling the story about how her supervisor copes with the problem by getting a lateral transfer that she has been looking for.

Interview

I was the first female to come to work in the prison and when I started, I had a lot of problems with the staff. For the first six months I was only hired on temporarily. I was replacing a man who had a heart attack and they didn't want to hire me at all, but the Women's Rights Commission stepped in and said, "Look, she is qualified." So I walked into a lot of problems when I started working here.

I didn't know anything about this at the time, but the security people tried to stop me from getting the job. The first two weeks, fine— I was just new and I was working with Al, and I was following him around and I wasn't doing anything on my own. A few weeks later the doorbell to the offices rang and he was on the phone and I said, "Give me the key, I will go down and check."

That's how it started. Security saw me alone and they went right to the Governor and he called me in and said, "You are not to handle the keys. I don't want you working alone." I wasn't saying anything because I didn't know anything about the place. So Steve is just pulling his hair out because he needs a staff member up there. Finally, they gave me a minder and we were walking around all the time together. As far as they were concerned I was only on for a term of six months. They thought, well, after Christmas, we will get rid of her—no more problems.

But he never came back. So they had me there and they couldn't very well get rid of me and get somebody else back in, so they kept extending my term for three more months, three more months—and this went on until last summer when I was hired full-time. They let me drag for two years almost before they made the job permanent.

After Christmas, they thought they would get rid of me by taking away the minder. By that time, I had gotten used to the place and knew how to play their games. I went right through Security, straight to the director of Security. He said, "You can't talk to me, you have to go through Steve and he has to go through his boss and his boss said no." I said, "I want to talk to you." I said, "I have been hired for the job, I'm going to do it whether you like it or not. I have been here for six months and I have never had one problem with the inmates." Security was saying I was losing the keys and they were trying to stir up shit. Every time I was able to clear myself. Then they were caught. They couldn't get rid of me so they said okay. So finally, they decided to take my minder away. So I started and within three months, I was a dead issue—I was part of the woodwork.

Last summer, we had a staff training program and I was down there and we were talking about different things. I had Security down there and I said, "By the way, what is Security's feeling towards me now?" I never went out of my way to say hello to them because of the female-male thing. And in here, they were used to having females who were secretaries and who they went to bed with so I didn't want them to look at me that way. I thought unless they talk to me, I won't talk to them. I really didn't have any feedback as to what they thought of me. So I asked them about their reaction to me now that I'd been here a year and a half. They said, "When you first started, we resented you. We used to say—if she gets raped, we'll just sit there and watch. Or we will jump in and rape her too." This is the language. I just couldn't believe it and now they said that 99% of the warders would be right behind me because "You have proven yourself." But you still have 1% of the old men who just can't accept females being in here.

I was pleased and there's no problem. I have the respect of all the Security. I am in charge. I have had inmates going to the director of Security to try to get one of my decisions changed, and they have called me down and I have told them the story and they say, "Okay, you are in charge." They never change anything on me or play dirty tricks on me. I never had a problem after I proved myself but I have to keep on proving myself every day.

Now that I have been working here, I can see their point. Although they shouldn't have gone as far as they went. I know when I have a new staff member coming in and I look at the person and think, is this person going to give me a hard time? Is it going to be someone I have to baby sit or look out for? Is it going to be someone I will have to clean up messes after? And until that person proves himself, then I don't let on. Then okay, no problem and I can go my way. But I have done that too. Well, they were scared. I was the first female and they didn't know how the inmates were going to react.

After I came, someone started working in the community centre or chapel and no problem there. After that, we had another woman who started working in the canvas shop last winter. Then we have secretaries in all the different shops—about three or four out in the population working. So seven or eight females in the population right now. Then you get all your nurses who worked there already but they were never counted as women and for some reason, they were just a part of the woodwork always. They're nurses—it's not the same thing.

I am supposed to be getting all these fantastic people in, and programs and entertainers in for the inmates—that's my job. But in fact, it's very, very hard to do for a lot of reasons. First of all, you have the mentality of the inmates to contend with and they are not open to new ideas. For them, entertainment is a jazz band like Dutch Mason and wrestling or things like that. They are so conformed in that it is very hard to bring anything different in because they will just walk away.

Right now, I'm trying to organize a field week the first week of August. I thought, Christ, let's really do something different. I have stacks and stacks of papers with my ideas on it and then I went to the Inmate Committee and I said "Okay, this is what I have. Let's see, and at the same time let's compare what they had before." They had last year's program and they went through it and said, "Okay, we are going to do this, this and this." Basically it's like wrestling, weight lifting, novelty races, kinds of things. So 1 said, "Okay, that's fine but how about something different." And 1 started throwing in my ideas. Like possibly getting in a mini-carnival. Well, they liked that idea but well, we can only win stupid toys or stuffed animals. The prizes weren't what they thought they should be. 1 said, "Okay, fine." Then 1 said, "What about something on the line of let's get a fiddler in, let's get some old people in—somebody who can square dance and let's have a country and western day."

"Well, that would be good for the old inmates but not for us. We are too young."

1 said, "No, don't be silly—that's fun. You will get into it." They don't have that open-mindedness that people on the outside have and it's hard to do something with them. So we have that problem.

Then on the other side, we have a security problem which is a real concern in this—you know, it's a maximum security prison. This morning, 1 had a meeting. 1 have a few events that I'm bringing in, and the problems begin. Okay, I'm bringing a magician in. Where do we put him? Do we put him out in the yard—all alone with the inmates or in the gym? Then 1 have a fortune teller who's coming in. Where do we put her? 1 have old people coming in. Where do we put them? The staff doesn't want to do it in the gym because we are scared to death. The inmates would harass us, and although they wouldn't harass the old people, they could take them hostage and believe me, we wouldn't have anything to stand on. They really wouldn't take them hostage, but there is still that possibility and we have to look at that.

And then there's the problem that the people from outside don't want to come in. And you can't blame them so it makes my job very difficult because I'm getting pressure from the inmates to bring people in. I'm getting pressure from the administration saying, well, that's your job, you better get people in.

No volunteers come in here on a regular basis probably because this is a small town. We used to have a bridge club. We used to get old people in to play bridge with the inmates. They just loved it. Then the old people decided they weren't coming in because the inmates were dirty—they weren't washing. 1 assume probably something happened to one of the visitors somehow and they stopped coming in. And that ruined it for everybody else.

It becomes very frustrating. I have had people come in, like the Canadian Cancer Society. They have a program that's about cancer for men. I thought, hey, fantastic. I put posters up: FOR MEN ONLY!! I tried to seduce them into coming up. I got nine names out of 250. Five came up and two of them played chess, two giggled and one actually listened. It's very discouraging for me and very embarrassing. Maybe that's my own personal hang-up because I've invited this person in. After a while, I think why should I bother, but then I get back up and say, well, it's my job, and I get back into it. But it's hard.

Yesterday, to organize the meeting we are having tonight, it took me an hour and a half just on the phone and that was to find one person who's supposed to be coming in to pick up toys that the inmates are making for children with learning disabilities. That's an hour and a half plus there's security, passes to go out and they want some food and on and on. For one movie which lasts from 6:00 to 9:00, it has taken me almost half a day to organize it. So when you are talking about a meeting a day, it's a lot of work and I can't do it alone. I just can't.

Before I worked here I graduated from high school and then I took a dressmaking course and I worked in my own shop for about a year. Then I went to Montreal where I worked for about three years. I worked in factories, I worked in a shop, and a restaurant. I really didn't know where I was going. Then I came back here and fooled around another year. I worked for Brunswick Furriers and at health salons. Then I went to university and took social services and I graduated. All those four years I went to university, I worked at the City Recreation Department. Then I graduated and started here in August, so I really didn't work at anything like this before.

Now I find that I don't like working with the inmates. I find them . . . how could I explain this? I like the work. I get along very well with the administration. And I get along with my bosses. I like the pay and the working conditions, as far as I am in charge of my own department. But I don't like working for the inmates. I wish it was for another clientele that I was putting all this work in. And I get very frustrated and pissed off and I think, Christ, all this money and all this time we are putting into inmates and there are more deserving people out there—like the old people, the crippled and the children. These people here have killed, maimed, robbed and heaven knows what all, and they are getting three free meals a day, a clean bed, clean clothes every week, a canteen, and they are getting paid and have recreation and entertainment. And they still complain and they still bitch and it's still not good enough. I get very frustrated at times.

It used to drive me crazy when I heard those doors close. Working here all the time, you are always in contact with the same people and whatever affects another staff member, affects you very much too. If you know a staff member is being harassed, you think oh, oh. I will probably be next. I was harassed from the middle of February until quite recently. Even the correctional investigator came in. Things like that get to me.

I had this cleaner and he must have been in the centre for about a year and a half. Normally I have close contact with my cleaner because he has about an hour or hour and half of work, and then he comes up to the office and he can sit there, and of course you would get to talk to them—it breeds familiarity. Finally, he started to fall in love with me. That didn't bother me because other inmates had fallen in love with me before and written me love letters. I would just kind of say it's just infatuation because I'm the only female. But because he was working so close with me all the time, he really couldn't get that out of his mind. So I started saying, "Look, maybe you should find another place to work."

And he said, "No, not really, believe me it won't get out of hand. It's just my own thing."

"Okay, fine if you can handle it."

It just got worse and got to a point where he would listen in on my telephone conversations and butt in if I was talking to somebody else. He would read everything I had on my desk. He really started to take hold of me. He wanted to know when I was coming to work and when I wasn't and what I was doing at night.

This had been going on for a year almost and I said, "You have got to find another place to work. It's just not—we are just not hitting it off." We started arguing and it was very ridiculous.

At that time, he was supposed to be going to the farm (a lower security component of the prison) so he was saying, "Don't transfer me now because you will hurt my chances of going to the farm."

So I said okay. There were always excuses why I shouldn't get rid of him. Finally, my grandmother died and I learned about it on the Monday and I left Monday afternoon. I didn't come in on the Tuesday and I didn't tell him. I mean, I never even thought of telling him. When I walked in on Wednesday, he was just ripping mad—just furious.

From there, the whole thing just went to pot. He started accusing me of all sorts of things and I said, "You are just going to have to get another work location." At the same time, I was going out to the city for a week to take a first aid course.

When I came back, they had taken him out of the community centre. He was putting charges against me—that I was playing poker with him up in the community centre, that I owed him thousands of dollars, that I had brought stuff out and brought stuff in, and I had forged cheques and heaven knows what else. When I came back from the first aid course, I walk in and this is waiting for me. And because of this Security thing, well, you have to prove he is wrong. I said, "Fine, take your job and shove it. I am walking out."

It just insulted me—the fact that I have to prove he's wrong. What happened to this you are innocent until proven guilty kind of thing? That doesn't work in here. You have to prove the inmate is wrong or else you are guilty. That's the way they go. That way they figure if you can prove you are innocent, he can't charge you with that again. So, I was quitting, I was walking out of the whole thing and then they said, well don't, stay on.

So I worked out front awhile. I was getting all this feedback from the other staff. The inmates were saying I was a chicken and that in fact, I had something to hide. I thought you bastards, you are not going to get to me. No way.

So I went back in and the cleaner came up to me and asked to see me and I said okay. I tried to talk to him and it finally got to a point where he threatened he was going to send somebody to my place to beat me up, and I found out who it was. With Security, I was able to find out if in fact it was going to happen. I didn't stay home that week.

Then he said, "Okay, if I can't beat you up or can't get you beaten up, I will get your job."

Then everything I could do—it didn't matter what I did—it was wrong, it was bad. It was terrible. To come to work was terrible. And I was going to Security and they said there was nothing they could do. I went to my boss and there was nothing he could do. Then they said maybe they could threaten to ship him out but in fact, they couldn't because he's not a security problem. It just went on and on and on. He managed to get all the rest of the inmates against me. Heaven knows what he told them. The inmates started calling me "bitch" and "pig" and saying, "There goes the rat" and "There's the slut." It never happened before and that didn't help the situation.

Finally, the correctional investigator came in and talked to me and I told him the story. He told me to forget it. This inmate has a record of rape and the whole thing. That's fine. The correctional investigator can say it's over and administration can say they have handled it, but I still have to go out there and deal with him and the rest of the inmates. So in fact, it isn't—it's still not resolved.

I am having a meeting tonight with him, with the group of which he is president. Heaven knows what he is going to come out with and what he is going to accuse me of. It's still not over. You hope that maybe it will die down and he will start picking on somebody else. There's nothing you can do. For me, I am a very proud person and I've never been subjected to abusive language on the street. It's not part of my environment. And to come here and be called that when I am walking through the dome and it's full of people, I mean, I just could die. The fact that there is nothing you can do about it just makes it a hundred times worse. Like, if you could turn around and say, "You. Down in the hole!" or whatever. But you can't do that. You charge him and then they are going to ridicule you and then he's going to lose five days recreation. So what? It doesn't solve a darn thing. So I find it very hard.

What I am trying to do is to show everyone that in fact, I have never done anything to deserve what I am getting. And they have always had meetings and things. And what I am doing right now is making bloody sure that I don't fuck up any of their plans. I go out of my way to make sure they get the meeting; I make extra sure they get the passes and that they know about it. If there is anything they want and they know I can get it, it's just a matter of pushing a little bit harder so I will do it. I guess I'm sucking up to them to put it bluntly, but I have tried everything else and it doesn't work.

Now if I can get them back on my side and then they could say, well Christ, well this inmate is saying she is so bad but how come we are getting everything we want. So maybe she is not as bad as that. That's what I am trying to do but I don't know if it is going to work. They follow whoever is waving the flag.

I have had inmates come to me and say we agree with you, so and so is really a pit. And then during the meeting, he tells me to shut up. He has put me down and they sit there and don't say anything. Well, they can't because I am a staff member and if they take sides, they are going to get their faces beaten. I have nobody really to help me in the population. I am just going to have to do it myself. I don't like it.

You can't trust them. At the last meeting, we had outsiders and this prisoner stood up and just made a complete fool of me in front of all the outsiders. And it's lies and the inmates know it's lies, but they can't say anything. But the outsiders don't know. There's a few that's come to me and said, "What is going on? It doesn't make sense." I have tried to explain to them what has happened but they can't do anything. Things like that make you bitter. It turns you off.

Finally the doctor took me off work. He doesn't want me to work here at all. He took me off for five weeks and he said "I don't want you to go back." I said, "Fine, I'll send you the bills. I have to live—I have a house, a car—I just need the money." So I am trying to find something else. But again, it is very difficult.

I guess I am at a point where I am doing my work and nobody else seems to really care, so why should I? But I can only do that for so long. I can't do that because I do care. I do care about the program and I do care about the field week—not because it reflects anything on me, but it is my work and my responsibility. I have been going to my boss to find something else. "Give me a lateral transfer, give me anything."

"No, no."

I came in on Monday and he said, "By the way, I am leaving in two weeks because I can't handle this place. I got a lateral transfer."

I almost hit him.

REHABILITATION ATTENDANT
Home for Children with Severe Intellectual or Physical Disabilities

Comments

He is a young man in his twenties with an easy way about him. He wants to get away from the kids for a while, so he's volunteered to talk to me until they go outside. As we talk, his frustrations emerge about the children and about his own place in the institution.

He says that there are many ways of looking at the hospital, so many values, and he presents several approaches to it—a kind of drug-culture mysticism, a strong religious ethic, and standard institutional dogma.

The mistrust of authority which comes from the drug culture lets him clearly see the harm the hospital does. He sees how hard it is to be humane to the children. He sees how the system is coercive without seeming to be. He recognizes the hidden brutality for what it is.

He says, "You take the kids outside in winter and play snowballs with them. You line them up on the lawn and throw the snowballs at them. They love it."

He recognizes that there is little change, little improvement among the patients. He puts much of the blame on the system, but he also believes that everything and everyone can always improve. This is a dangerous belief to have in a long-stay hospital. It carries with it a dark side. If patients do not improve, if they don't change, or if they regress and deteriorate, then who is responsible? It cannot just be the system. Obviously someone is not doing it right.

His religious ethic leads him to assume responsibility for not improving the children under his tutelage. If only he did it properly, he somehow could make it better—make the children better. This tension between the pull of omnipotence and the hopeless impotence of failing to achieve success is a dilemma. He says, "You can take it as your responsibility and say well, what the hell is the matter with me, I can't seem to get him to improve any more. You can say, I'm doing nothing.

All I am doing is changing diapers."

He also abides by the institutional mores although he distances himself from them. As much as anyone else, he is prepared to shut up and get on with the job. He learns to ignore many of the difficulties in order to survive himself.

So you have to go with the system—you have to look out for Number One or pick up your pay cheque and find another job. If you want to be rebellious—that's what it comes to. The only thing you can rebel against is to leave the system. You can't beat it.

The cost is his fear that he himself is being institutionalized. The hospital is lulling him to sleep. He has escaped from the real world into this very secure, very stable place where he has few responsibilities but is not really developing. He is becoming like the patients. "You feel you are being looked after. It's so big that you are like one of the children yourself. It sort of rolls and you roll along with it—that sort of thing."

Interview

I am a rehabilitation attendant, even though I'm trained to be a child care worker. An attendant is classified as a non-professional caretaker of the residents; whereas the child care worker is a paraprofessional. Here, the problem is that it's a very closed system. There's very few child care workers in ratio to the staff population. I guess it's about, off-hand I would say 10%. Well, this is going to frustrate the worker because there's no chance for psychological or monetary remuneration. You just sort of reach a dead end and eventually with time, it's very easy to take the attitude, "I don't give a damn, I don't care because they are not caring." If you are not cared about enough, there's a burn-out point.

Child care workers don't really have much more of a role. Becoming one wouldn't make a hell of a lot of difference in power. People would have to listen to you a little bit more, simply because you are one rung up the ladder, and they would be afraid because you have the power to report them if they don't toe the line in some shape or form. Status—a certain amount of status. Monetary security—again that comes into it. That is sort of my plateau—to better myself. This is my new Utopia—to get this far. Basically, I think it is the financial. An attendant who has been here for 25 years is making the same bloody pay. In 25 years, there's no chance for a raise, where at least a child care worker can accumulate seniority and an education, can get to a certain plateau and earn decent money, which is all I want. But you are constantly blocked if you don't get to that level, and Western society is certainly geared to a certain amount of status.

In my philosophy, I try to get away without what I am speaking now, but it's coming out to you. That's really how you have got to play it. That is what's really deep down. You always want more no matter what level you are at. If you are a doctor, you got a lower status if you are working with kids with intellectual disabilities. The brain surgeon is the big shot. The brain surgeon will look down on the G.P. who walks around here playing with bells and hitting knees and reflexes and things like this.

Still, there are people who stay in these jobs for twenty or twenty-five years. It would be interesting to take all these files and get some sort of reason why people stay in the system for so long. There are a lot of fucked-up people in the system. No question about it. You are going to hear different reasons why: "I love the kids"; "I love the system"; I love feeling secure"; "I don't know how to do anything else"; "I am thirty years old and I can't change now." The reasons are as varied as humanity.

Many people who have been here a long period of time are so institutionalized they are not ready to change themselves. They fear looking elsewhere. Because there is one thing that institutionalization does give you that I think is very important: it gives you some sort of sense of security—that you are part of something, you feel you are being looked after. It's so big that you are like one of the children yourself. It sort of rolls and you roll along with it—that sort of thing. You just go with the waves. You keep your mouth shut when you have to and just keep going. Change is so slow and things seem so stable that you get this feeling of comfortability, really. You can feel really bad but you go home and the next day you come in and everything is beautiful and peaceful. You are not out in a restaurant hustling all the time. It's a slower type of life and you could maybe weigh that point and look at it. I'm not getting ulcers over it for the most part. I think, again, maybe I'm not going anywhere. If your ambitions are to be a great man and to have fame and fortune, this is not the place. Thinking about Krishna-murti or something like that and say, the bigger you are, the further you have to fall. You can sort of come back.

I have been here not quite two years. I came here off the street needing a job, and after some months of working on availability, that sort of thing, I said, why stop and just be an attendant. Why not get some education so that you can work with basically any type of population and you have the paper to show you are qualified to do it, without having to know somebody? I'm enrolled presently in a program that trains child care workers and other paraprofessionals. I enjoy it. I think it's quite informative. I don't have a big yardstick because I haven't gone to university.

Before this, I was a jack of all trades—farming, construction, landscaping. I like this work now. If you are going to classify humanity, you could say that I work on the ward for the lowest grade patients and I must say, I was a little bit taken aback but it all depends on your value system. I said to myself, somebody has got to take care of them, why not me? I am not in a position to say, "How can I take this? These kids are nutty and there's going to be shit all over the place and this is what I am going to do for a living." That really didn't enter into it. I think it takes a special kind of person, be it into sadomasochism or whatever. Because I've seen people come in and start running for the door. They are freaked out. It's normal. There's always a level of freaking. It's just if it's for you or not. I believe a lot in fate too. I think that at the right place and the right time, you come for a job without really knowing what is going to be your thing, and you fall into it.

I have fallen into my thing. This is it for the conceivable future. Maybe that's institutionalization, I don't know. I guess that part of it is probably the whole Protestant work ethic—that you have got to settle down and have some sort of profession that you can at least be secure with and fall back on, even if you decide to change later on. There's something you can do, and it says somewhere that you can do it. I think that's very important for me right now—the education and the experience working in this place.

Basically, this is their life. The residents don't have free society here, where you can go and do what you please. They are really dependent on administration for any type of activity that they may want to do and even then, when they get it, it is not usually what they want to do and it is organized for them as a group. It's good for, let's say, group interaction—something like this and to be able to do things together. But there's not too much freedom of choice for the individual. Follow the sheep as they go and that sort of thing. On one unit, I believe it's called B, maybe it's now J-1 (at times, we are so institutionalized, I can't remember it—I am used to the old system), I think they could have more autonomy than they do now. There again it's a question of staffing plans, problems like this that enter into it. Who wants to put out that kind of bread?

You have got about sixteen residents and you've got about four staff so we have to organize it in a way that everything is done by everybody. If it's exactly what they want to do, you would need a one-to-one basis which isn't very feasible. That's the way I see it. But usually when there's outings, not everybody will go. All the activities, except for eating and things like this, are things that everybody can do together. For instance, tonight there is an outing to a ball game. Usually you will get a select group that gets to go and you will have the other ten left out. Tonight it works out very well. Most of the kids are home with family, on holiday or whatever, and there's only about four or five residents in the unit so they can all partake, but this doesn't apply when they are all here.

There's really no choice. The regulation department says we are going to do this and we are going to do this—like it or not. You pretty well got to go anyway. Even if you say, "No, I don't want to go," you will be convinced to go. I think the residents are more or less brainwashed by the system. And the staff is too. Definitely so. In a situation of the staff—child care workers, rehabilitation attendants—your own suggestion doesn't go over very well, even on a consensus of the staff. It will be heard but you are at the mercy of the unit head for your wish to be carried out. It still comes from the top and you are not a doer, you are a follower. That's how I regard it. Say a resident doesn't want to go to a ball game and you say, "Okay, you don't have to go if you don't want to"—you may be reprimanded by your superior because you don't know how to properly socialize or handle him. Or you'll be told that the resident isn't going because he doesn't like you and perhaps he doesn't want to go with you. You are sort of on a teeter-totter. You got to please your superiors as well.

There has to be some sort of organization but I don't think there is as flexible a lifestyle for the residents as there could be. It is not moving towards normalization. Yet, however restrictive it is in here, we need structure for responsibility. If we don't have any restriction of freedom in the name of being responsible people, perhaps we will all become delinquents or handicapped or disturbed. The preferences of the residents can't be met because they are so dependent. That's their problem. They can't walk down the street by themselves.

It's very, very difficult for the individual worker but you can have a little bit more, say a little bit more power, if you get along with the consensus of the various cliques . . . power cliques. If you cross them and somehow things are a little rougher for you, you are bucking the system—very similar to a prison. You get the strong arm tactics—bend a little bit or we will bend you, same sort of thing. Sabotage, during the last contract negotiations, one guy got sugar put in the fuel tank. Or if you get on the wrong side of your supervisor, then they can change your hours. So you have to go with the system—you have to look out for Number One or pick up your pay cheque and find another job. If you want to be rebellious—that's what it comes to. The only thing you can rebel against is to leave the system. You can't beat it.

A lot more could be done because first of all, people are very good in this institution. There are close checks by the administration but when the administration is not there, I think there is misuse of the kids. Staff, in time, tends to become frustrated and take out their sadistic tendencies on residents. It's under the covers, you don't see it. Bumps and bruises and foot marks on the kids—you don't see it happening. The evidence is there so there's still the same old stuff done on the sly. There are also the new and funny ways, you know. You take the kids outside in winter and play snowballs with them. You line them up on the lawn and throw the snowballs at them. They love it.

I haven't done much reading on the subject of how things have changed over the past few years. I know that things have improved since the 1850s but the same type of philosophy employed by society then is still around—that society must be protected from the insane or criminal and they must be locked up. This hasn't changed. Look at rehabilitation—who is going out of the institution and making it? Nobody. I can say everybody is getting better. They say this because they test someone on some scale or other and he has improved. Sure, it looks beautiful on paper. Nobody is in here to check and see if it is true, or what it means. Who cares? I don't think things have changed. I think living conditions have improved in the past century or two—there's no doubt about that. It's not full of cockroaches. It's clean and the kids are well-cared-for physically and mentally as well as the system stands.

I don't think, looking at it psychologically, there's a lot of change. I think the idea of punishment before reward is still credible. It's so much easier for us to look on the negative thing rather than the positive, and the results are certainly much more evident to see. If there is some sort of physical punishment inflicted, we get to see the results. The psychological is very hard to measure and again it is measured by paper. It doesn't necessarily have to be true. You are making a conference for a kid and it will be presented by a written document and presented to a panel—who is to say how accurate it is? It may be just for a feather in one's cap, for status in the eyes of society, and to get rid of frustration and this sort of thing in general. That's the way I see it more or less.

It's very difficult for me to say how a kid really improves. I think there is a bond that grows between two people—that sort of thing. Well, basically there is more good vibes, more eye contact, more embraces. I'm just talking very generally. I can feel those differences. A stranger walking in would never get them. I think feeling comfortable both ways, trust in a relationship . . . but as far as actual improvement educationally for these kids, I personally have not seen too much. I don't think I've seen too much.

Their education is handled by education department teachers and we constantly hear reports that a kid has improved. Yet on the unit, we see the same antics, the same type of compulsive behaviour that goes on day in, day out, year in, year out. And I'm taking that from staff that's been here much longer than I have. But where is the improvement? Johnny has been the same way since I have seen him. I haven't seen any change. Perhaps there are changes but perhaps they are so clouded we don't see it. It may be so minuscule. He may eat better. You expect that of a three-year old child. He attains that level and basically stays there. Perhaps he hasn't gone on to the next step in his learning process. You can take it as your responsibility and say well, what the hell is the matter with me; I can't seem to get him to improve any more. You can say, I'm doing nothing. All I am doing is changing nappies. It's so slow that you don't even see it and what has changed may have been five years before you got here and they have stagnated since then.

Again, I think that the kids are so dependent; they are paralyzed to be independent. Their physical disability creates this dependence. I think there has got to be a way to have more independence emotionally. To be able to do what you want because this is their home. It's so geared to "Do what I tell you" all the time. But if you leave the kids awhile, sometimes they fight with each other and they can't get along so you have got to step in.

Again, the question of economics. If somebody smashes Johnny's face, then who is going to be responsible? Who wants to be sued? All of a sudden, the parents are great lovers of the children and wanting $30,000. You got to protect them—step in. You are like a prison officer at times.

And changes are few and far between. Any transfer of unit here that takes place, most of the kids don't know what is happening. There are some who can talk and these types of residents would be aware of it but where there is no verbal, it's hard to measure. I don't think they know what the hell is happening. When a staff is moved, they would know the difference from their usual caretakers. But mostly they would be out to lunch. They would miss them a bit but that's about all.

It's hard to tell about moving kids around. There's situations, for instance, where we are going to have this guy separated from his brother because they try to hold onto each other and don't get any work done—this sort of thing. Then they are back together, then they are apart. Decisions there have been made, been reversed, but there's really not too much changing around. It's news when it happens. "Oh, did you hear about so and so moving downstairs?" It's a big thing. He's a lot of work. It's usually not a treat for somebody to go somewhere else. It's usually somebody with some sort of physical problem and for some reason or other, there's the wish that the kid will be better off in another setting. I can't even say if it's for him to be better off.

Another example is a schizophrenic kid, who has another kid who will interact with him. He will take his hand and start whacking it on his head. It seems to stimulate him. He seems to like it. He's craving it. He loves it. If you take him and put him in another unit, who's to say— maybe somebody else's hand, you don't know. They have been so perfectly matched and classically conditioned for years that it is like apple pie and ice cream. That blond brat, he would do it to himself, but maybe the other one wouldn't get him going so maybe his behaviour would improve slightly—his acting-out behaviour might diminish.

There's an experiment somebody could do but it wouldn't be very fair to the guy.

I know that I'm stressing on the negative and I just can't say at this time what can be done to ameliorate the situation. There are so many value systems.

REGISTERED NURSE
Long-Stay Ward
Psychiatric Hospital

Comments

She is a small, reserved woman from the Philippines. She is very uncertain about this place and about her work here. In response to the question about what it is like to work here, she tells me about the day in great detail.

The description of the schedule sounds like a mixture of scientific procedure and religious ritual. The minutiae of the day in a total institution are carefully worked out and meticulously followed. Every event has its place in the day. Rooms are locked, opened, locked again. Patients are fed, washed and medicated at prescribed times. Everything follows these procedures. She says, "If everything goes according to routine then we accomplish what we have set out to do, and it's a good day."

But the day is also full of the peculiarities of institutions. It is an open ward, but the patients are locked out of their bedrooms during most of the day. The day begins at 6:00 a.m. and lights-out is at 9:00 p.m. Events are interrupted by medication times and meals are at institutional times: breakfast at 7:00 a.m., lunch at 11:30 a.m. and dinner at 4:30 p.m.

She is not so sure what it is that she has set out to do; she is sure that it is not nursing. It certainly isn't like the nursing she did in the acute-care hospital where she worked before coming here.

Here she is a nurse for patients who need no nursing care. And she resents this. She resents not only her own lack of productivity in this job but also the patients who do nothing, who are so dependent and who are not productive. "I have a hard time to treat them like persons, like regular persons." What she is angry about is that they do not really need her care. And this means that she herself is not productive. At the end of the interview she concludes that: There is no nursing care. The patients are healthy. None of them are really bedridden. When they get sick they are transferred to the infirmary. It's that three-story building at the other end of the hospital. This ward is their home, unless they become sick.

Interview

I don't mind the work here. Sometimes it's nice, especially if you are able to get through to them, and you reach your goal. But sometimes it's so frustrating because everything you do is useless, and it's so disgusting and painful because you are trying so hard and you don't get any response from them. If I had my choice I would like to be an operating room nurse or a general surgical nurse, but since I have been here for the past year I don't mind it. I don't think that I would like to stay here for more than three years. Then I will go back to the general hospital. I have no plans to change right now. But the other kind of nursing is more interesting. There are always changes in procedures, and new techniques to learn. And you can see the patients change. When they come in they are so totally helpless and you do all the care for them. And after five or six days, they are better. They are up and ready to go home. You can see their progress. It's very nice. Here there is no change, it's the same thing every day. It can be rewarding for a week or so, but then it becomes bad.

We have one charge nurse in the two wards, and she has 62 patients altogether. There are only two nurses working on each side, for 30 or 32 patients. So the most staff there are for the 62 patients is four, five, or some days there will be six.

We start work at 8:00 a.m. We take the reports from the night staff, and then the charge nurse makes the assignments. She delegates the work: giving baths, morning care, and then supervising those patients who are really capable of doing things on their own. So between 8:30 to 10:00 you give your morning care. Then everyone has to leave their room and the rooms are closed and some of the patients go to Occupational Therapy (OT). Only around ten patients are supposed to stay here. This is an open ward, so most of our patients come and go as they please. Some of them work in the OT Department. Some of them go and sit in the cafeteria, and help clean dishes, or set up the food, either in the staff cafeteria, or in the patients' cafeteria. But most of them, they just stay in the ward and enjoy themselves by smoking, and many enjoy drinking coffee.

I have a hard time to treat them like persons, like regular persons. Some of the patients have talents, like they can play piano and we have a piano here. We have some patients who can play the harmonica. Almost half of them just participate in their own ways. It's up to the staff to let them participate and function at their own capacities. Up until 11:00, they're having their rest or coffees, and then at 11:00 it's medication time, and then someone goes down to the cafeteria and gets the lunch trays for the patients who can't go downstairs by themselves. At 11:30, one staff goes with the patients for lunch and the other stays on the ward. Between 12:30 and 2:00, the rooms are opened for the patients so they can rest. The patients who work in the OT room usually leave by 1:30 and we close the doors to the rooms again at 2 o'clock. The others sit in the day room and watch TV. After our break at 2:00, we see who leaves the ward to go to other supervised activities.

In summer, we have lots of activities for them. Our open ward is, of course, very active. We take some of the patients and go swimming or bowling in the recreation centre. Only 30 patients can go to these activities at one time. But really there are less than ten from both wards who go regularly and who participate. They don't all spend their time on the ward. Some of them will go outside by themselves. You know, they lie down in the sun, or go for a walk. And also during the summer, the charge nurse arranges outings. We go to parks and have picnics, we go to museums, and we even go to Washington. And only a few who are very bad stay on the ward for those things. We also have barbecues and things like that. So they enjoy that.

At 3:30, we check to see who is gone from the ward. Sometimes they really disappear because this is an open ward. So we just check those who are awake to know their whereabouts, and then we prepare for the change of staff. When I am on day shifts, I leave just before 4:00. At 4:00, it's medication time and at 4:30, it's time for supper. After supper there is usually a movie or a dance, and some of the patients go to these activities. But others just refuse to go and enjoy themselves by staying here and sitting down and watching TV. At 7:00 o'clock, they usually go for the dances. Sometimes there are volunteers who come here for bingo. Or sometimes the band plays a concert and they go there and get free refreshments, as an inducement for them to go. On a warm evening, some of them will go outside for a walk. But if the weather isn't good, they'll stay in the day room and some of them will play piano and do some singing, or play games. There is also evening care. Some of the patients are not capable of doing their own personal hygiene, and so we have to do it for them. Those that really need the most care, we do in the morning. And those that need just some supervision, we do their care in the evening.

We do our main census at 9:00 o'clock after the main doors of the hospital are closed. We check and if there's a missing patient, we call the nursing office and we search for them. If they can't find them, they go on Unauthorized Leave. There is a special form for that. We have to inform the police and everything must be done according to specification.

They get their evening medication just after 9:00 o'clock, and we open their doors. After that they're free to go to bed. They usually go into their rooms between 9:00 and 10:00. At 11:00 o'clock, we have to make rounds so that we are sure that they are all in bed, and then we prepare the last reports. At midnight, the night staff comes on. There's only one staff for 32 patients overnight. The problem is that you have to make rounds all night, and you are alone if anything happens. Then at 6:00 in the morning, they wake the patients and give the first medication. The patients get out of their beds. And at a quarter to seven, one staff goes down to get the trays to serve breakfast to all 62 patients, and the other stays on the ward. And then they prepare for the changeover to the day staff.

If everything goes according to routine, then we accomplish what we have set out to do, and it's a good day. Medication is at 6:00 a.m., 11:00 a.m., 4:00 p.m. and 9:00 p.m. But in between that, sometimes if they're disturbed or agitated then we also give them medication as necessary. We have tranquilizers to calm them down. They go high as a kite sometimes, and they could become very agitated or restless or very loud, and then they can be physically or verbally aggressive towards other patients and staff, so they get them as necessary. But it's not very often that that happens in long term cases like these because you know the patients, and you will know when something is about to happen and who is really to be looked at carefully. Like when they are starting to get dressed, we have to check their vital signs and you can often tell—sometimes some of them are affected by the drugs, and their blood pressure goes way up or down. If their blood pressure is off, then we have to adjust their medication. And we have to sometimes be careful not to give them too much.

They have their ups and downs. Most of them have been here for a very long time. Somehow they change. When they first come in, they're calm and quiet. But after five or ten years, some of them begin to shout and get agitated. Our most long term patient has been here for almost his whole life, over 45 years. He started in the children's ward. He is 51 years old. Many of them have been here for between 20 and 25 years. Others as long as 30 years. One woman came in when she was in her early twenties and now she's 65. She has schizophrenia. Most of them have spent over half their lives in here. Most are in their 50s, 60s, and 70s.

You will find some who are not really very sick mentally. They could really go out and be outside. When they started to stay here, this became their home. But it's better than home—they don't have to wash dishes and they don't have to cook. Once they become candidates for foster homes or group homes, they start to act up, so we cannot send them out. Our goal really is for them to go out. But it is impossible for us to send them outside because whenever we see that they are able to go out, we tell the social worker that they are ready to go outside, but when the social worker comes, they start to act up. They are not suited to go out because they start to become sick every time we decide that they can leave. When we actually get them out to a group home, they become violent. They have to cook, fix their bed, clean up and so on. Here they just have to sit down and wait, and it comes to them .

In here actually, they don't do anything except smoke, eat, and sleep. We do everything for them. If they tell you "Open the door please!" we are there to open the door for them. When they bathe, we give them towels, face cloths, soap, everything. We are there. Almost half of them are stronger than us and really could work for a living. Some of them will come back from the cafeteria and say, "I stopped working." So I ask, "Why?" and they say, "I only get small pay, like a child." Actually, they pay them to work in the cafeteria, but it's really a motivation program. It's not the payment but just a way to motivate them to work. They know that they get money from the government, so they're content with that. They get enough for their coffee and cigarettes. Everything else is provided for them. They don't even have to wash their own clothes. They just send it to the laundry. So there's nothing for them to do. Everything is fixed. We clean their lockers for them, their bedsides. It's a first-class hotel. But they don't pay for it. The government even gives them an allowance.

I've only been here for about a year and a half. As I go out the door, I take it all off. It has to go away. I don't want to think about them at all. You can't take it all seriously. You can work as hard as you like and sometimes you don't get any reaction from these clients. So it's up to you, if you want to be convinced by them or if you want to convince them. At home, I sometimes think that if I stay with them for their care for ten or twenty years it would harm me. Every day you come in, with only two days off in the week, and you are dealing with the same persons, the same faces. So in your mind, what will happen to you to be exposed to them for so long? What will happen to you? You are human after all. Would you believe if I tell you that there is a patient here who was a nurse here before? It happens. So it's up to you. You know the consequences, what can happen. So that's why, like me, if I go out of the hospital, I don't think about them. I enjoy myself. Because after ten years, you or me could be one of them. It depends on how you take it. If you become so seriously involved with the patients, you have to put so much of yourself into them that it's impossible. If you're so emotional and so sympathetic to them you can go crazy. There has to be a kind of wall between us and the patients.

Actually, really I am so close to our patients. I always sit down with them, talk to them and everything. I think just two people sitting down and conversing normally is how you have to get through to them to gain their confidence. They have confidence in us. If the regular staff is off sick or something happens and a new staff has to fill in, their reaction is different. They become so insecure because they don't know the person that is working. Sometimes they turn the other way around, and show their back to the person. Instead of cooperating they become resistive and very uncooperative to the new staff. They don't know them. If it's the regular staff, they go along with you, not all the time, but at least they feel more secure and comfortable.

We don't have any favourites here. If we did and one client noticed it, it would be bad. Some patients tell us that we are too firm or hard with them, and I think that it's because of their type of personality. There are some people that you can look at calmly and quietly and just talk normally. But others if you talk to them normally, you can't get through to them. You have to raise your voice a little bit and be firm so that they will follow what you say. And some of them really offer help to us. For example, one patient always is near the nursing station and she will offer to go down to the cafeteria to get some lemonade and other things like that. But it can become hard when she begins to ask for cigarettes, and there aren't any around. Then she will get excited. If she starts that you just have to ignore her and sometimes she'll calm down. But she stays near the nursing station all the time, and if there is a float on she can be a great help because she can show you where the patients are and so on. She has been here a long time. Much longer than me.

When you come to work here for the first two or three months, you are really a newcomer and the patients don't listen to you at all. I used to work in a general hospital in the surgical ward, and then in a nursing home. Here it is different work. There is no nursing care. The patients are healthy. None of them are really bedridden. When they get sick they are transferred to the infirmary. It's that three story building at the other end of the hospital. This ward is their home, unless they become sick.

NURSING AUXILIARY
Geriatric Wing
Long-Stay Hospital

Comments

Her feelings about the patients and their situations are complex. She sees them as adults and as infants. They are full of wise lore and they are "sweet." She says that their death makes her sad, leaves her unmoved, makes her feel guilty, and sometimes results in relief. But the overriding feeling seems to me to be one of despair. These long-stay wards are filled with people waiting to die. This woman and others like her are in an environment suffused with this despair. And they are prepared to look anywhere for hope.

She both accepts and denies the reality of death. She is frightened of her own hardness, but her work reeks of death and disability and her response to these things. Her concern with death pervades much of her conversation. She is not easy with her work. She is not sure if it is appropriate to treat the patients as infants, but it is a good way to think of them nonetheless. Is it good because it makes it easier for them or for her or for their relatives? At the end, she talks of a boy with physical disabilities who through sheer effort of will has managed to regain some of his abilities. She seems to be asking if we could do that with old age and death.

Is there a dignified death to be had in institutions? What does it mean to lose one's dignity? A large part may have to do with an unchangeable routine and one's high degree of dependence on others. A nursing assistant in a nursing home described the morning routine in which she changes the sheets and washes the genitals of all her patients.

Often the loss of dignity is harder to recognize. It can come from attempts by a demoralized staff member to lighten the atmosphere for themselves. This woman and her colleagues have tried to "normalize" the ward by dressing the patients in clothes split up the back, and doing their hair and by dousing the male patients in aftershave. But the result is that they transform the ward into a grotesque doll's house in which the patients have become playthings, and illness and infirmity are unsuccessfully disguised.

Interview

I'm a nursing auxiliary, I work with the patients. I have nothing to do with the medications but I give them all their other care. We feed those that can't feed themselves, and the ones that can feed themselves—we encourage them, keep after them, coaxing them along. We bath them, change them, toilet them. Total care—we do everything for them. I like it. I worked on the wing for children with intellectual disabilities for four years, but I like the old people better. Maybe it's because at the time my own son was a baby, and I was never away from kids. I worked with kids, I'd come home to kids, and he was a problem child too. So I went over to the old people and I was scared. I didn't think that I would like it, but I really like it. I like helping them. I like fixing them up—like the old ladies—we curl their hair, and put their hair up and dress them up. One time all we put on them was gowns, but gradually we asked their families if they couldn't bring in dresses and split them up the back. So they could be dressed and make them look nice. You take a pride in it. If they look nice they feel good and we feel good because they do. You know yourself if you lounge around all day in a dressing gown or pyjamas, you feel yucky. Whereas if you get dressed, it gives you a lift. Or if you get your hair done, it gives you a lift. And I think they feel the same way. Even though they're old, they still think about that. Age has nothing to do with it. The men, the same. Keep them shaved, cut their hair if they need it cut, fix them up, put a little after-shave on them, put them in their clothes.

Most of them have cancer or heart problems. Most of them are confused. Most of them can speak, and there are days when they're not as confused as other days. Nine days out of ten, they're confused. And one day you go in and they're making sense, which is a shock because you're not expecting it. Then the next day, they go right back again. You just go along with them.

They all have ways of communicating. It's a lot like kids with intellectual disabilities—they have ways of telling you what they want. Sometimes it's with their eyes, or a certain move—they have their ways. If you know the patients, you can communicate. We had a woman who was a Hungarian, who had come over for a visit, and she had a fall or a stroke, and they brought her here. She couldn't speak a word of English. We communicated with her. She was just the sweetest thing.

The suffering is the depressing part of it. Terminal cancer patients are very hard to see on a day-to-day basis because it's long and drawn out, and they really suffer. There's nothing much you can do for them except keep them clean and comfortable. You see them come in— they're a good size when they come in, and you see them go right down to nothing. That gets to me every once in a while, especially death, when they get close to death. We have a woman now on the floor and she could go at any time. When she first came in, it really bothered me, and I like her and she was friendly and everything. But I got so I found I was not going to her too often. I would walk by and say, "Hello, Mrs. Brown," and I'd keep on going. I knew it was wrong and I knew that I shouldn't do that. It's death. It's not the patient that you're shying away from, it's the death part. It's something that no matter how long you work in a hospital, you don't get used to.

I've worked around death for a long time and I can remember the first time that it didn't bother me when someone died. This woman was here and she died and it just didn't bother me that she died. I thought that was terrible. I was really upset because it didn't bother me. I thought to myself, "Am I getting that hard? It's about time that I got out of this." It was quite a while before I realised that I couldn't stand to watch her suffer so terribly, and now she was out of her misery. So it wasn't sad to see her go. I went to a couple of seminars on death and dying. I was always scared of a patient asking me if she was dying. You're not supposed to lie to them. But I don't know if I could tell someone that she was dying, just say, "Yes, you're dying." Because you don't know what they want to hear. At the seminar, they said that you should come right back to them with the question, "Well, what do you think?" or, "What has the doctor told you?" That's helped, but so far no one has said, "The doctor has told me that I'm dying," or anything like that. I don't know whether I could deal with it. Most people are scared of death, I guess. We don't face death. I often think about what I would do if a doctor said to me, "Betty, you have cancer." I don't know if I could face that. Maybe it's also the suffering. Especially if you're not around it, you don't know what it's about and to know what to expect isn't always a good thing. We see how they suffer. We see how long they can suffer, and it's almost unbelievable how they can still go on.

These people have bad hearts, they're supposed to have heart problems. How does their heart ever stand it? I don't know how it holds out. I don't think it's just the death part. It's also knowing how long you're going to suffer. This seminar we took was terrific.

It's not only cancer that can become pretty awful, there's other things. When a sore becomes gangrenous, the families have to sign a consent form. Many of the patients are not capable of signing for themselves if they have to operate. And if the families don't sign, then it just progresses. We don't run across that too often, though. We do see a lot of sad things. The worst is that we see more go out on stretchers than we see walk out. In some ways it's not the worst about it because when they go out, they're not suffering any more.

They really suffer, even if it's just arthritis. Arthritis can be really painful. And tumours, even if they're not malignant, they do damage. One woman has a benign brain tumour. She's sad. She had a young daughter, and she was scared that she wouldn't get to see her own granddaughter, but she lived to see her. She has a hard time talking. She knows what she wants to say, but she has a hard time getting it out and she gets very frustrated. Sometimes you try to wait, but sometimes you sort of help her along and it makes you feel kind of bad, but you have to because you don't have the time to wait. And at times she's grateful for your help. But she's always sorry. She's always sorry because she has trouble standing and you have to take most of her weight, and she's sorry for that but she can't help it. And she's sorry that she takes so long to get things out. And you feel guilty because you can't spend the time with her that you really should.

Everybody's good to them. They're given good care. At times you forget and you don't treat them as adults. You start to think of them as babies. We've talked about them like that. "Our babies," we say when we talk about them. And in a way, they are babies. Naturally they're somebody's mother, somebody's grandmother, they're adults. But in their minds, they're babies. There's an old saying, "Once an adult, twice a child." And I really believe it. Now that I work here, I see what it means. So many of them go back. They're always calling for their mothers, calling for their fathers. Very seldom do they ever call for their sons or their daughters or their husbands, unless they're around all the time. Even in some cases, they don't know that they are their sons and daughters.

There's a lot of trouble with the relatives. In some ways it's good, and in some ways it's not. I believe that the families do have the right to complain because if my son or my mother or anybody was in the hospital, I know that I would want certain things. And if I didn't like how he was being treated or how she was being treated, I would say something. But sometimes they want you to do something that interferes with Mother's health or Father's health. When it comes to them telling you or telling the hospital, or the nurse, or whoever, then I think they should be told, instead of saying, "Oh fine, we will go along with the wishes of the family." The families should be taken aside and I'm sure if someone explained it to them, they would understand. But instead, in many cases they just go along with the family. Maybe they say, "Mother can't take that kind of pill," but Mother has been taking it and it works fine. Or say, "Mother should stay in bed," but lots of times it's not good for Mother to lay in bed because the lungs fill up. You have to sit up to break up the phlegm and mucus, but because the family wants Mother in bed, we leave Mother in bed to make the family happy. To me, that's interfering with the welfare of the patient. And if they come together on some kind of decision about what to do with Mother, I don't think it should interfere with her welfare. I don't really think that they mean to harm Mother. That's why I think it should be explained better.

Some families though are trouble. The least little thing and they run into the office. I think that you should take people like that aside and have a little meeting with them and the charge nurse. There is nothing that prepares the relatives for what goes on in the hospital.

When we get a new patient, the family should be shown where the Green Room is—that's our sitting room, and they should be shown the Sun Room. And they should be told that when the patients get up, they will go to the Green Room or they will go to the Sun Room. That's where most of the activity is except for singsongs and TV-watching. Everything else is in these rooms. I don't know what they tell them when they come in. But the first day, the patients get up and we take them to these rooms. And their relatives come in to visit, and Mother or Father isn't in their own room, and all hell breaks loose! They go running to the nurse, and they don't want Mother there and they don't want Father there. If they were prepared for the shock of finding an empty room, then maybe this wouldn't happen. Naturally, in a hospital like this if you see an empty bed you figure, "She's dead!" or "He's dead!" Or think that something terrible has happened. All these hospitals are like this.

There's a lot of things that we should have, like there are no activities for the patients and so they just sit. Even though they're not going to live much longer, why should they just sit? Sit in the corner, sit in the chair and look at the wall, or look at a TV when there's things to help their mind be a little more active. This summer we had a bit of an activity program and it was very good—they got out once in a while.

Some are active by themselves. We've got one lady, she's always on the go. We call her the Roamin' Catholic or the Wandering Jew. She laughs. She likes to joke. She goes out every Sunday when her family comes for her. She had a cold one time, and we tried to talk her in to staying in that Sunday and going to bed. There was no way. Her daughter took her. She didn't take her too far. But she went.

If a patient will fight you, really fight you, we like that. I don't know if it's true but we feel that as long as they've got the fight, they've got the will to live longer. That fight means a lot. We've got some that are like that. They'd as soon give you a fight as look at you. We've got one old lady up there that if you go to do anything with her, she's always pinching you and saying, "Get away! Get away!" She's pretty well crippled up, she's practically curled up. And she sings. She loves to sing. But she's hard of hearing and she's really something. Boy, when she sings, she really bellows it out. And she talks a lot of the past. A lot about her childhood. How she used to sing in the choir, and how her mother didn't let her sing until she was twelve so she wouldn't spoil her voice.

We used to have one old lady who'd tell you different things. She was an intolerant old thing, but she had a mine of information. Like if there were buds on the trees in the wintertime, it meant that there would be a poor harvest. And if you made rice, then scrub your rice together and it takes all the starch out of it. She'd tell you different things like that. A lot of it was true and a lot was old wives' tales. If you were stuck on something that you were going to make for supper, you'd go in and she would give you all kinds of tips. I think that we gain more than they do in a lot of ways. We get to learn an awful lot about the old days and how things were.

I remember one old lady we had and she was really funny. She was from the country and she never had any education. She used to tell us that "Dad used to sit under the tree. And I ploughed the fields." And this I believe. "This one time," she told us, "Dad had a bottle and I dumped it out, and I ran like hell down the road and he was right behind me!" Someone was talking about a sword, and she said, "Yes I sawed the horse's ass every time I ploughed the field." It was so funny and so sweet.

We've had patients here for years—four, five, six years. We remember them. We often talk about the ones that were here a long time before they died. The things they did were sweet, because they're like kids. If they say something that's really catty we think that's really sweet, really funny. Everybody has their favourite. Glenda is mine. She has an intellectual disability. She just had her birthday yesterday—she's 32 or 33. Most of the girls favour her, but I do especially. She was 26 or 27 when she came, and it was supposed to be temporary. Her mother was dying and her dad put her in here. Her dad is just terrific with her. He comes in every day, and he takes her. He may just walk her around in the building, or if it's nice, he'll walk her around outside. She's either in a wheelchair or a geriatric chair. But she knows. She knows strangers. She knows a lot. She doesn't talk because of her disability. She's failing now. She's lived past her life expectancy, and she's failing. She becomes depressed and stops eating every so often, about twice a year. But once she starts to eat again, she'll get better and there's no stopping her. She's been going downhill for the last couple of years, she could go any time. I don't know how I'll feel about it—if I'll be upset, or if I'll be glad to see her go because she has been sick for the last while. Her health hasn't been up to what it was. So I don't know how I'll feel. There's been other women who I've been attached to that died and most of them it didn't bother me, and I thought it would, and that's another thing that bothers me.

Most of them are very old and sometimes we forget that they've gone through life, with a family and with kids. And when they come out with something, we find it funny and sweet, and maybe we shouldn't because they're adults. And this is something that we always forget—that they're not babies, they're adults. We're taking a course that they're pushing. That they keep saying that they're not babies, that they're adults. They don't want you putting ribbons in their hair they don't want you giving them dolls. But in some cases, like there is one woman up there who wanted her baby. Her husband went out and bought her a teddy bear, and she cuddles it just like a baby. And she said she wanted more because they'd had three. He went out and bought another one, and she said, "Well, there's one more to come." Another woman, she was very sick one time, and she kept crying because, "They had taken her baby away." And we just couldn't quiet her down, and she was quite sick. So we got a doll and we wrapped it up and gave it to her and she settled right down and went to sleep.

And we had a woman who one night was screaming and screaming and screaming. And we went in and asked, "What's the matter?" She said, "I'm having my baby! I'm having my baby!" She was literally reliving the birth pains, and when she quietened down, it was over. She had had her baby, a baby boy. It's really something. A lot of funny things happen. One time another woman was screaming, "I'm having my baby!" And we said, "You're not having a baby." She said, "Yes, I'm having my baby." And I asked "Well, what are you having?" And she says, "I'm having a baby goat." And she had a black goat.

We get some patients that give you a really hard time, not just an acute time but a very hard time. And we've been told that if a patient begins to really get to us, so that we feel like we are going to snap at them or argue with them, then we should go out of the room, leave them, and report it to the nurse. It could be our fault or just that the patient is ugly, miserable. Sometimes a patient that isn't confused becomes upset because they're in here or their families aren't coming. There is always a reason behind it. So the best thing to do is to go away—leave that patient, go do another patient. You can't just leave him. If the patient has to be restrained, you restrain him. You don't just walk away, but you don't carry on working on that patient. Then maybe if you calm down and he's calmed down, you come back or you send somebody else to do him.

Some days we really get frustrated, we get tense and tired. Mostly it comes out when you get home. Like the first person who says something to you, gets it. Or else you snap at the other workers or at the nurse. Everybody's careful not to let it out on patients. I think that we give pretty good care. I don't want to pat myself on the back or anything, but I do think that most of the staff is caring. The odd time you may scold a patient, and then you feel like a real monster because it's not the patient's fault. But maybe it's been a bad day, maybe the nurse has given you a hard time. And that's why when you're working with this type of patient, you shouldn't have to work under tension because you've got to be happy. You can't be tense because if you're tense, whether you say anything to the patients or not, they can feel it by your touch, they can sense it. Like, maybe you come into a room and you're quiet, and you just do what has to be done and say good morning. Usually you come in and talk, and spend some time with them. Well, then they get tense too. And they might begin to give you a hard time, or get weepy or snappy themselves. Sometimes there must be cases where a patient is turned a bit more roughly, and things like that. But you don't see that.

I often think that it must be terrible to be so dependent on other people. A friend of mine has a son who's nine and who was very active. In fact, they thought that he was hyper. And he had an accident this winter that left him crippled—he had a blood vessel that burst in his head. It didn't affect his thinking. In fact, he's brighter than what he was. And he shocked the doctors right along. It happened right after Valentine's Day. And they thought he'd be a vegetable and they wanted to put him in here in the kids' wing, and Shirley said no.

He was dependent, but he wouldn't have it. He's not now. The other night he said he wanted something to eat out of the fridge and Shirley said, "No, you've had enough." So he got himself right out of the chair in the living room, and he sat down on the floor and he edged himself to the fridge and he was in the fridge. It's a real miracle what that boy's come through. He shouldn't even be alive with what happened to him. And if you would see him now, it's just unbelievable. Now he wants to walk, and the doctors just don't know, because they didn't know he'd come this far. By bringing him home, he's been able to do this.

I say and everyone says that if he had been put in an institution, he wouldn't be where he is today. Different times he gets upset because his mother is tied down. She can't go out. She has to be there all the time. She has to walk him into the bathroom, put him into the bathroom, put him in the tub. She used to lift him into bed, and she told me that one night he said to her, "You know if you got that foot stool and brought it here, then I could crawl into bed by myself." The first time it took him twenty minutes or so. But now he does it by himself all the time.

CHIEF OFFICER
Super Security Unit
Maximum Security Prison

Comments

I was waiting for this officer to finish doing some paperwork when loud shouting suddenly came from one of the subunits of the cellblock. He raced out of the room and came back a few minutes later with three burly warders practically carrying a small, skinny inmate who was yelling and holding the side of his face. The inmate was shouting obscenities, "They didn't have to get rough with me, the bastards. They just are fucking goons! They go after you for fucking bullshit!"

He sat down beside the inmate and told him that he had to behave, that he was going to send him back to his cell to cool down and that would be the end of it. The inmate was led back out of the office and the interview began.

He is a balding man of 32. He managed a high street shop before becoming a prison guard. He coaches sports and is involved in other organized recreational activities. But he "never has become involved with an inmate."

The disparity between work life and home life is especially great for workers in total institutions. At work there is an intensity of violence, pain, illness and deviance. At home there are wives, children, friends and a community. Workers try to separate these two lives. This compartmentalization between "inside" and "outside" is meant to protect home life from the horrors of their daily work. They do not want to bring the nightmare home. This is not unusual: we all try not to bring our work home with us. And we hope that we will not bring the problems from home to our work.

This man puts a lot of effort into separating his home life from his work in the institution. Even though it is common for warders to take on double shifts for extra money, he is careful not to work too many hours.

He will not fall into this part of the work culture. He tries to keep his relationship with colleagues and inmates business-like. And to this end, he does not befriend inmates or socialize with the other warders.

One effect of this radical split is that life in the prison becomes less than real. He no longer sees that the horrors of his work happen to real people. He stops seeing them. He is like Walter Mitty who also had two lives. Walter Mitty's fantasy life gave him dramatic power and violent action, but his everyday life was prosaic and domestic. This man has genuine power over others and works in a world of violence and action. His fantasy is that all this is not happening to real people and that the only reality is prosaic and domestic. He brings this tidiness and domesticity to his work world. He says:

> Maybe it's that I fish a lot and all that. I clean fish, but I stand there and watch them cut their throats and slash and everything in front of me and it's never bothered me but maybe I do blur it. A lot of times, I don't see faces. I just see a body.

And he ends by describing, with some disbelief, the things he sees (but ignores) in this real (but fantasy) world of the prison: homosexuality, sexual abuse and perversion.

Interview

I came upon this job by sheer coincidence. I was working in retail management and I was managing a shop in Penolia at the time. I was working too many hours. I said to myself, "This isn't for me." So I just quit. I came back here with the wife and kids. I never had a job. I went down to the employment office and I said "I am looking for a job." They said, "Have you thought about becoming a prison guard?" I said, "Well, not really." They said, "Well, they are holding interviews this afternoon. Would you like to go to an interview?" So, I said, "Sure, why not." So I went down to the interview, and I was sitting there in the interview room. Apparently nobody knew I was coming because the Appointments Board were leaving and they seen me sitting in the waiting room and they said, "Are you for an interview?" And I said, "Yes I am." So they called me in and all the time they were asking questions I seen one guy in the corner going through a bunch of papers, and he finally speaks up and says, "Have you filled out an application form?" And I said, "No."

But anyway, I received a letter a week later. I was hired.

It was a whole different world. In those days, you never went on a course first. You started right in the institution. The Staff Training Officer gave us two weeks induction and from there, we started getting posted. You never even had a uniform so I went around approximately eight or nine weeks without a uniform and that put a lot of added pressure on me because the inmates knew I was fresh and green. We had very, very low training—you had to learn by yourself. You had to make sure you understood your orders. I guess I coped with it.

I've been in the service for nine years and in this prison for a little over three years. I worked at another prison for six years as a guard and was promoted there to senior officer. When I came here I was promoted again to become a chief officer. I have been in charge of the Super Security Unit since January.

The only way an inmate can be placed in Super Security is, first of all, he has to harm either a staff or another inmate, or he has to be involved in a hostage-taking. No street crime will put you in Super Security. It has to be a crime within the institution and of a serious nature. This prison has got the worst inmates from all over. Then your Super Security Unit has got the worst of those.

This is the place for inmates who have done their worst. After this place, there is nowhere else to go. These five subunits are the end of the line. When I say this is a Super Security Unit, I mean three of the units are for Super Security. One is Protective Custody where inmates are placed for their own protection, like sex offenders or guys who for some reason or other are going to get killed if they stay in the general population. The last one is Segregation—that's the hole.

So actually I'm dealing with three types of inmates in one unit. A part of my job is to make sure none of them mix because if a Protective Custody inmate mixes with either one of these two, he is dead. And then the Segregation inmate, if he mixes with the Super Security inmate and they are together, they figure they got more muscle or more pull, and then something eventually starts so that's all got to be monitored as well.

Now we have to monitor all the inmates here—every time they go into the yard, when they go to common rooms, when they take showers, what they eat, and who they hang around with. We have to monitor all these things because this is all fed into a report that is done semi-annually for the Review Board for inmates who are in Super Security. We do a Segregation Review Board every thirty days for those who are in the hole. I am a member of it, along with the governor, the two assistant directors, plus socialization, security, classification and recreation people. We have to make decisions.

All the inmates who go in the hole, go in on my count. They are my responsibility and I have to monitor them and there's a lot of times where I'll take a guy out before his time—sometimes because there is no room and other times just because he has been no problem since he's been there. Let's say he is sentenced to 21 days. Well, if he hasn't said boo in 15 days, I will say, "Okay, you are out." Hopefully that works in the long run because when he comes back he's not going to be a problem. When you work in that hole and the 16 cells are full, all it takes is for one inmate to start pounding and then the other 15 back him up.

For the inmates in Super, there is a phased program that they go through. They start off at Phase 1 where they get one hour's exercise a day and that's it. They graduate from Phase 1 in approximately two months depending upon good behaviour. Then they go to Phase 2, where they get just about everything. They get one hour exercise a day, they get common rooms at night, and they get a TV in their cell which no other inmate room has. They have a gymnasium that we built right in the unit. From there, they still have approximately six or seven months again depending on good behaviour, before they move to Phase 3. The ultimate aim of Phase 3 is you are out. You are back in the population. But not in this institution. You must go to a Maximum institution population elsewhere and they try their best to send him where he wants to go. So an inmate can conceivably only spend 12, 13 or 14 months in Super and then he's out. Now there are inmates who have been here for four years because they just won't conform. They will do everything they can to stay.

It's home to some of them and sometimes they think of themselves as martyrs for the rest of the inmates. They are the big hero because they think, "I've been in Super Security for four or five years. I'm a big hero. You guys got nothing on me." When they do hit population, they are treated that way too by the other inmates. They say "John is a nice guy. Give him a carton of cigarettes. Give him this. Give him that. He spent four years in Super Security." As a matter of fact, the inmate in

Super Security, except for the freedom of movement, has it better than any of the other inmates. But yet these inmates out there will try and send in stuff left, right and centre for these guys. I don't think they really realize how good these inmates have it. They got their own TV so they can watch TV 24 hours a day if they want to.

Since I have been in charge of Super Security, I work straight days. I'm here all the time, doing all the paperwork. I have two teams—18 men in each and they alternate afternoon and day shifts, and then the staff members who work in other parts of the institution come in here for the midnight shift after they are all locked up. So it's just doing rounds then and monitoring all movement. There is some animosity between the guys who work in here and the other guards in the institution. I guess it's because the guys here don't do the night shift, and they are only responsible to me and not to every other chief officer in the place. I also think that this work is much less boring than sitting and looking at inmates from the end of a row of cells.

I am very, very busy right from the minute I start in the morning until the minute I quit at night. I have a population of 74–75 inmates at the present time which is far, far too many for a Super Security Unit. Every inmate that is escorted out of this unit has to be escorted by two guards and they very seldom leave this unit. We have medical facilities right down here. Our interview rooms are here for different lawyers. All of that has got to be coordinated and priorities have to be set because it is just impossible to do them all and paperwork is a real pain in the ass. I have tons and tons of paperwork I got to keep up every day or I find myself getting behind. Now the paperwork I'm talking about are enquiries that have to be done, grievances that have to be answered, or letters from inmates. I got to look after 36 men's annual sick leave. I got to keep all their records up to date daily. Things like this. That's my daily program more or less but it's always interrupted as you were just aware of.

Now there's a guy who weighs what? 70 pounds soaking wet. But he's got to prove himself a big man or whatever—I don't know why they do it. So my day is interrupted like that constantly. We have various things like fires. In the last couple of months, we have had two attempts at hostage-taking so that takes up a whole day—everything else gets put aside. You have fights. You have a group of inmates who get together and refuse to come in from the yard, or refuse to go into their cells or whatever. So you have all these things daily which inter-feres with what you are supposed to be doing.

Still, I like the job. I like paperwork. I like making decisions so I get to do that—I get involved a little bit now in decisions and policy-making. I also like the action part of it. There's a lot of action—espe-cially here in Super Security and I enjoy that. I don't know if that is good or bad really. Don't get me wrong—I've never hit an inmate yet, I've never had to. But if there's an emergency situation, I like to get involved. So I enjoy that. I learn how to cope with different situations, how to deal with different situations, when to make certain moves and when not to. It's all experience and it helps. Chief Officers are in charge of the institution on the afternoon and back shifts so in actual fact, they are the warden for that period so if something comes up, they have to make the decision.

I've got to watch the inmates a lot but I've also got to watch my staff a lot too. For example, I got to be aware if I see one of my staff mem-bers becoming really tense and uptight. I will call him aside and tell him to cool down. Let's say a minor incident just occurred and then another one or three days in a row go by, and I see he is just walking on pins and needles. And I know damn well that he's going to blow up at the next incident and I feel sorry for the guy standing in front of him. I try to make myself aware of that. I say, "Have a coffee, have a cigarette, stay there for an hour and come back." And maybe talk to him—tell him to cool it. I say, "You got the rest of the day to put in." I ask, " How many days till you are off?" or "You want some annual leave?" Or what-ever and then I get him out of here. I don't want to lose him because he's a damn good guard. The men who work here are damned good but there's times when it gets to that point.

I know a lot of people that would like to quit here but the money is too good. With the overtime, there are staff who make more money than the governor. There's a lot of overtime if a guy wants to work, but then again you will find that your alcoholism is high, your separations are high—the reason is because the guy is never home. He gets that extra pay and next month he wants to double it. Some guys handle it well. Some guys in two years' time got their home paid for already but some people can't do that.

Now, we had a chief officer who died last night of a heart attack and he is one of the best-liked men in this institution. He was only 34 years old and he is dead. He looked about 30—a very young guard, but he's dead, probably overworked. The only outside interest he had was his fireplace. That's all he talked about. He put in a whole new furnace. As far as exercise or playing sports or anything, none of that stuff. To me, that didn't help. There's a man who was very well-liked. A young man who had everything going for him. He had a good future ahead of him. He was sure he was going to advance in the service. He's got the wife and two small kids. He had a beautiful home. It was just gorgeous. Now he's got nothing—it's too bad.

I worked strong for one year and that was it. I haven't worked over-time since, except in emergencies. But then I got a lot of outside inter-ests too. When I go home at night, I try to forget about my whole job. I'm involved in sports and everything else. I coach kids. I play myself so I've got something that takes it off my mind, but there are staff that don't and they must lead a very difficult life. I don't hang around with anybody from the prison because I make a point of it. None of my friends work in a prison because I don't want to talk about the job when I'm away from it but when I'm here, I really enjoy the work.

I don't think the change from this place to outside affects me. When I leave here at night, I walk out that gate and it's a half hour drive for me to go home. It loosens me up driving home. I start thinking, "Okay, I got a ball game tonight or a hockey game." The wife, she has made the odd comment that, "Where do you think you are, at work?" But then I start thinking, what am I doing? I don't think it affects me but maybe it does and I'm not aware of it.

Maybe when I discipline the kids, I sometimes am affected by the work—let's say one of the boys is doing something and I start disciplin-ing him. I would hate like hell to have one of my kids end up in jail, and I hope none of them ever do and I keep emphasizing that fact to them. I try to tell my kids what it's like in jail without really getting into it.

I never talk about my job to my wife, especially in this place, because you got inmates upstairs that all they do is slash. We got inmates upstairs that got slash marks from here to there, and there to here. They just stand right there in front of you and say "Watch this!" Then they slash themselves and blood is flying all over the place. So I just don't talk about that kind of stuff to the wife, but maybe I have been getting too severe in disciplining my kids—I don't know. It's just that I become extremely angry if I do discipline, and he turns around and does it again. It irritates me.

Like that inmate just now—we sat down and talked to him and he calmed down. And then again, if he pulls the same stunt tomorrow, well then I'm not going to sit down with him. He's going to go back into the hole. I believe in giving everybody one chance. I will give him two chances but no way do I give a third chance. I just wash my hands of him. I say that's it, no more—I'm not talking to him.

There's very little inmate contact here in this unit unless you have got the right amount of staff. Whenever an inmate is escorted, there's two men on him. Now, in other Super Security Units, when they move an inmate, he is moved in leg chains and handcuffs. We don't do that. We got some of the toughest inmates in here. You name them, they are all here, and other than their threatening and that, they have been no problem. Now they do stab one another eventually but I don't care about that as long as none of my staff is hurt. If an inmate wants protection, all he's got to do is ask for it. If he doesn't ask for it and maybe he gets knifed or whatever, that's not my problem. That's the way I look at it.

They can kill each other off and I'm not saying that facetiously, as if I hate them because I don't. Now I don't like them, but I've bent over backwards a lot of times for inmates. As a matter of fact, I get run down a lot for doing that but I play the game. If they are good with me, I'm good with them. If they cross me, I cross them. If they got a problem, they sit down and talk to me, so I must be doing something. They know if I say no, they can go higher than me. But they won't sit there and argue with me. I'm the type of guy where I disagree maybe with this program and I'll be right dead against it. But then again if the higher-ups say, "This is the way it is going to be and this is the way you will implement this," I'll say "Fine, I'll do it." I might be angry for a day or two.

Most times they go to the governor and he says no and then they come back to me, saying, "The governor says no, can you help us out?" As long as you realize it, it shouldn't bother you. Then they are using me. I get a kick out of it at times. I will play one against the other. I've done it. Sometimes it's advantageous to do that.

I don't really think I despise any of them. I really don't. Now there's times of the day that I do. I will see so and so standing there, and if I could kill by the law, I would kill him. But then there's other times that same inmate (it could be an hour later), I will be talking to him. It's hard to explain. Often they are blurred in my mind. I do that a lot I think.

I've never become friendly with an inmate. I don't want to know what he's in here for. There's a lot of people that work here that's up in the records all the time. I never go near them unless I'm doing an inquiry or something where I have to know. I don't want to know. If a guy's a killer, I don't care what he is. The only thing that will really upset me is when he really crosses me, and that only upsets me for a period of time and then I forget about it. It's the old standard cliché. I must get threatened once a week and I will just shout back, "You will have to stand in line, there's about five of them ahead of you." It doesn't bother me.

What really shocked me since I've been in this area is the amount of blood. I always thought it would really bother me. Maybe it's that I fish a lot and all that—I clean fish. But I stand there and watch them cut their throats and slash and everything in front of me, and it's never bothered me but maybe I do blur it. A lot of times, I don't see faces. I just see a body.

There are other things in here that you don't normally see. Like homosexuality—everybody asks me about that. It's true, it's there. You always hear this is that inmate's kid, that's so-and-so's kid. You live with it when you work here. It seems to me that homosexuality is especially prevalent in maximum security prisons—I don't know why. It's probably because they have been in the longest time. They wouldn't be in maximum unless they were doing long time.

I shouldn't say that. There's one guy, he never does more than two years. Whenever he comes in, he's always in maximum just because of his attitude. He's just a punk, that's all he is. He's a native of the town. But most of your inmates in maximum institutions are doing life.

When I see them walking in the front gate, I feel sorry for them. I really do but then after a week goes by or whatever, I don't feel sorry for him because as far as I'm concerned, "If you can't do the time, don't do the crime," the old cliché. I have gotten into arguments with people outside the prison, I will say, "Look, the guy did the crime, he was sentenced for it, that's his tough luck whatever happens to him." And I firmly believe that.

I see Bone, who's a new inmate, walking in through the front gate.

He's only a 16-year-old kid. I know exactly what will happen to him. He's either going to conform to their wishes or he's going to be in protective custody. Either one. Nine out of ten conform. They got no choice. It's not as bad as prisons in other places, where you got your gang bangs. You don't have that kind of offence. If a young kid attaches himself to one older inmate, that's it. Nobody else can touch him because they know if he does, he not only has to contend with his father, he is going to have to contend with everybody else. That's not the case everywhere. Here they just stick to one person. It's usually a big muscular bloke and that's basically why they probably do conform.

Staff have to ignore a lot of things unless it's very blunt and out in the open. If you see two inmates sneak into a cell, well you know why, and if you see it out of the corner of your eye, you are going to ignore it for a little while. But if they do it right in front of you, well then you got to do something about it because if you don't, you are an easy mark for them. Stuff like that.

The odd time an inmate will get punched in the mouth and you will turn your head because the inmate deserves it. You have heard of the inmate code and that's very prevalent out there. We let the inmates solve a lot of their own problems. It makes our job easier. It makes living for them here easier, to solve their own problems. I have done it myself. I've had inmates come up to me and say, "Boss, turn your head for five minutes." I turn my head for five minutes and then I see this joker with a black eye but he deserved it. He was bringing heat on the whole unit.

Away from here, I don't hesitate to tell people what I do. I say I'm a prison guard. Usually you get all your questions when you are camping or at a party, and you are meeting a lot of strangers. I don't mind answering and I'll even throw in the odd story sometimes without mentioning any names. Here's something that really happened.

I was on midnight shift and I'm walking down the cellblock on tier 4 and as I'm approaching, I hear matches striking. I see a flame of light and then I see it go out. I sort of wondered what was going on. I figured somebody is trying to start a fire or something. I hurried on down anyway but I was quiet—they didn't hear me coming and this guy is a real pervert. What he did, he got off on lit matches so what he would do is light a match and jerk himself off at the same time, and he did this night after night. He would just stand there, light a match, grab it, light a match, grab it until he came. People laugh. This is a true story. This guy is sick. There's no doubt about it, you see some pretty strange things.

ADULT RESIDENTIAL WORKER
Ward for Women with Intellectual Disabilities, Psychiatric Hospital

Comments

This institution was built almost one hundred years ago by convicts from a nearby prison as a hospital for the criminally insane. It is an enormous granite building that now houses five stories of adults with intellectual disabilities on the grounds of what has become a large psychiatric hospital. Although there are green lawns surrounding the building, no one is outside. Everyone is on the wards on this bright sunny day.

The hospital contains a concentration of adults with intellectual disabilities who have not returned to the community. One consequence of getting people out of institutions is that the most severely handicapped remain and are harder to care for. It makes the institution even more like a warehouse.

This place is a nightmare of institutional life. People are lying on the stone floor in various states of undress, or standing about alone or in small groups. Most of the staff are in closed glass booths at the end of the long corridors which serve as day rooms. There is a smell of urine and ammonia. It is very noisy. Some of residents are shouting to themselves, or moaning. Others are engaged in heated discussions which cannot be understood.

The administrator who walks around with me shows how they have tried to humanize the spaces by adding a living room, complete with a stereo and TV. But the residents have destroyed all the equipment and the furniture within a few months. The paintings are torn off the walls and the hanging plants are dead or bedraggled.

On one ward, I am introduced to a few residents who are special cases—a man with a burn-scarred face who is an arsonist, an especially old man with Down's syndrome and a very short, well-groomed nervous man with an oddly shaped head. The arsonist tells me that the short nervous man was a celebrity and world traveller. He has a rare syndrome and for many years he lived with and accompanied a famous professor on speaking engagements as a live model of his condition. Unfortunately, the professor died, so here he is. Everyone laughs at the story.

None of the staff have spoken to me until I return to the office. There I meet the adult care worker whom I am to interview. She tells me about her work in a very subdued voice, and only becomes enthusiastic when she complains of the incompetence of the administration.

Most of her talk is in the form of justification. She justifies the way the place looks and how the inmates are treated. In this way she is very much like the administrator: "These patients are as developed as they're going to get." Their "lack of activity seems to be part of their make-up." She can't do anything for these patients because no matter what she does, they resist; they don't want to do anything. That is just what they are like. There are too many barriers to doing anything for them. Anything would take too long. It is impossible.

But she is also against the administration. The system does not allow anyone to really do anything. When you do try to do something, you will get in trouble with the administration. The administration will not ever support you. The administration humiliates you and always takes the patient's word against the staff. The patients and the administration are in league to stop anything from happening. Finally, you end up doing nothing. She says:

> So what was the staff supposed to do? We said, "Let them do what they please." The administrators brought it on themselves. Nobody wants to lose their job. . . . So we're forced into a position where we just kind of let the resident go.

There are many suggestions that she herself is ashamed. She sees that the inmates are human. They know what is going on. She says, "There are things that the residents know before the staff do." She betrays a recognition of the casual cruelty common to institutions: "if you would come and stand back looking, you'd think we were terrible people." Much of what she says helps to allay her fear that she too is part of the system which gives these people very little care.

Interview

Mentally, the patients that we've got are children really but because of their age, they are adults. They are all ambulatory. There are adults with intellectual disabilities. Three or four of the patients are dealing with more mental health problems and their behaviour is more of a problem than the ones with intellectual disabilities. One of the girls is quite self-sufficient in self-care except when she's in one of her cycles, and then she becomes very dirty, and her old habits come back. She might sleep all day, she doesn't eat. Some of the psychotic ones get so depressed. We have treatments if they get really badly depressed, and we've had one girl who had to get shock treatments. Most of the patients are on drugs every day anyway to maintain them, but even so, there will be two or three times a year when they go through this bad cycle. But it will cure itself in time; you just have to wait it out. Almost all the patients are on drugs of some kind or another. For example, the seizure patients take anticonvulsants and muscle relaxants and so on.

They all like attention—there are the occasional ones who thrive on it. Just like children with intellectual disabilities, they like to be held and touched. At times, too much attention by one person can harm them because they get tied to one person and they'll do anything for that person. But if that person isn't there, they won't do anything for anyone else. So you have to keep a happy medium. I do kind of like one girl who's deaf and dumb. She thrives on one-to-one attention. So you have to give her enough attention to ward off bad behaviour. If you ignore her for too long there's ripping clothes, head banging, breaking windows, things you don't want her to do. For some of them, physical attention is the best reward you can give them for doing something. Cuddling and holding children is a lot different than cuddling and holding adults. It's been a long time since I worked with children but for these patients you just have to pat them on the back, or put your arm around them and give them a treat like a sweet or an orange drink while we're having our coffee. None of them smoke on the ward now. We did have one but she was a higher grade and she's moved on to a higher grade ward. We did have to light her cigarettes because she was a spastic. The ones who have profound disabilities have never been in a situation where they might learn to smoke. Their pleasures are food, drink, things like that. That's really what they look forward to—their next meal, a nice warm bed, and the outings that we go for. I don't really know if they have sexual lives—the ward is virtually all females. There is only one male and he's never had anything to do with females, so there is no sexual activity. But on mixed wards, there are some who have sexual relations.

These patients are as developed as they're going to get. As a result of daily repetitions in their routine they get to learn things, but don't look for anything to happen overnight and don't look for any drastic change. It depends on how high they function: what might be a small thing for one of them can be a gigantic step for another. For an autistic person, just paying attention to a little piece of work for a couple of minutes would be a gigantic feat, whereas for someone else that wouldn't mean a thing and isn't near what you should expect from them. It takes a lot longer for autistic people to develop any kind of attention span. There was a movie I just saw about an autistic kid whose parents took over treatment on their own when he was about three and it took them over four years, but they gradually got him started talking, he started school when he was seven. I don't remember how many thousands of hours that one of them took him into a room and they would spend the whole day with him. But then he was a normal child apart from his autism. Had he dealt with an intellectual disability too, then it would have been impossible.

I like my work, I enjoy coming to work. I like to take care of them. I think that's why I enjoy low grade residents as opposed to higher ones. They're happy with whatever attention you give them if they're lower grade. They don't know anything better. Many of them don't seem to realize that there is anything better. They're not always looking for something as the higher functioning [ones] are. They're a lot easier to work with. Although their capabilities aren't high, their willingness is there. For some of the higher functioning, they know what they don't have to do and sometimes they can give you a hard time.

The administration is especially bad here when it comes to their relationship with the staff. There are things that the residents know before the staff do, and they run to the administration with every little thing. If the staff does the least little thing, the resident runs. There was a case where a staff member was accused of having relations with a female resident, and it wasn't even witnessed. Still, he was suspended immediately. Eventually he was brought back but anything he had to say meant nothing. He could tell them the way it was, but the point was they didn't believe him. And they weren't willing to find out before they sacked him. That kind of attitude on the part of the administration has a lot to do with bad morale. I think that all you can do about that is to get rid of the administration.

Considering the type of administration they are, they are on the wards as often as anyone wants to see them. They don't make regular visits or anything like that. So the people that are dictating to us what we should be doing with this certain resident don't even know the resident. They don't even have an idea of what he could do; they only know what they want us to do with them. The people who assess the residents and make these decisions don't include us. We don't get into it. The residents are assessed and then they decide. They do let you work with certain residents by yourself; you don't have to ask anyone. But mostly, they expect you to do things even when you know that the resident might not be able to do what they want you to do. There isn't much training of staff in the institution and sometimes when they offer things like lectures or seminars, they don't free you from the ward to go to them.

I worked at Morrison Psychiatric Hospital for about four years before I came here. I liked the work there. There were so many facilities right there in the hospital. Everything was very well organized and everybody seemed to know what was going on, and there wasn't the confusion that I did notice when I first came here. The supervisor I worked for there stood up for his staff, while here everybody is so afraid for their own job that they won't do anything to rock the boat.

At Morrison, I worked for low grade male patients. They were adults, just like the females that I work with here. I have no preference for adults, it just happened that way. When I first started in intellectual disabilities, I worked in homes for special care. They were all children sixteen and under. Before that, I worked at other jobs for a few years. When I started at Morrison, I took a course in care for people with intellectual disabilities. They had you working on the wards for a few months on probation and then if you were selected, you took this course while you worked. It was a good way to do it because the probationary period weeded out the ones that weren't really going to stay anyway. We worked while we were taking the course, so I think that it saved them money too.

In institutions, you can't treat the residents like you do your own children. There are lots of times that a good spanking would be the best thing you could do. But you don't dare do that, because it would mean you would lose your job. So you put them in the corner. If they've upset

furniture, you make them pick it up. Make them clean up after themselves if they've made a mess. Sometimes if they're bad enough so that
they're going to hurt somebody else, then we have to seclude them
until they quiet down. But that's the difference between my type of
resident and the higher grade residents. The higher grade are bright
enough so that you didn't dare discipline them because if you did, then
they're knocking on the administrator's office door. They were going to
report you every time you turned around. And here are a lot of cases
where the residents' word is taken over the staff's. So what was the staff
supposed to do? We said, "Let them do what they please." The adminis-
trators brought it on themselves. Nobody wants to lose their job over
something like that. So they're forced into a position where they just
kind of let the resident go.

I would prefer that some of them weren't on the ward. But I don't
dislike any of them. I work with so many different ones. It makes your
work interesting because it's different every day. It takes a long time to
get to know all about a resident, about their behaviours and their
quirks, their likes and dislikes, warnings of bad behaviour coming. Or
seizure patients—you can quite often tell when one of them is going to
have a fit by their behaviour, so you watch for it. Our ward is quite
noisy quite often. If you come in for the first time the noise would drive
you crazy. But if you're in there every day, then you can distinguish
between the daily noise and the noise that something special is
happening. If somebody yells because there is a fit, then you learn to
pick that up above the usual noise.

We have some facilities for them, and some activities that they can
go to. There is a playing field and there is a pool at a centre close by.
There seems to be no motivation to do very much physical activity. We
take them to the pool and they put on their bathing suits and sometimes they'll go and stand in the water but that's about all. I think that
it would be good for them but this lack of activity seems to be part of
their make-up. Because of that reason there are a lot of our girls who
are in drastic shape for the age of them. We have patients ranging in
age from 17 to 55. The average lifespan of someone with Down's syndrome is about 40, and most of our residents are younger than that.

Those residents that are higher grade are exposed to a lot of public
facilities and public places, so they shouldn't shy away from leaving this
place. I think that lots of them should be put out of here. I don't mean

that we can just drop them back into the community on their own, but they should be able to function with some help in group homes and that. Some of them are bright enough to realize that in this place, they've got it made. Their food is supplied, their clothes are supplied, they don't want to go out into the community and have to fend for themselves. That kind of reminds me of people who could be your next door neighbour or mine sitting at home, on unemployment, just because they don't want to do anything. I think that the people in here should be sent out and at least tried. There are others being sent out who don't even have as good a chance to succeed.

There's an old fellow downstairs from us and he could have been out of here years and years ago but this is his home and that's where he's going to stay. He doesn't ever want to leave. Maybe it's the only permanent place he's known.

I think that a lot of it is that the public on the outside doesn't want them there. It was these people's parents that put them here, obviously. Very few people want to have a group home for adults with intellectual disabilities next door to them. And if the public aren't going to accept them, they are not going to make it outside anyway. One reason the public has trouble accepting them is that they don't look like someone they completely understand, and another reason is that you never know quite what to expect from them. You could end up with an arsonist next door to you and nobody wants that. We've got one right here who is badly scarred from setting himself on fire. He didn't do it intentionally. He likes fire but he didn't intend to burn himself. He just doesn't make any connection between lighting the matches and getting burnt. You really have to watch him. So there are real risks to letting someone like that out of here.

I'm sure that the administrative staff, if they were honest about it, wouldn't want them living next door to them either. You know that they have intellectual disabilities and everything, but you don't know all their little quirks. You don't know if you'll be robbed blind, or if you'll come home some day and find somebody sitting in your kitchen, or if other things like that are going to happen. Patients have done these things when they were living outside. That girl that I told you about who smoked—that's why her mother finally brought her in. She would just go wandering into anybody's house, she still will. I can't honestly say that there is anything that can be done about it. She has been running away ever since I've known her and I think she always will. She knows for a week or so that she's not supposed to do it, and maybe she won't. But then she'll do it again, and she doesn't think that she's done anything wrong. I think it's fine for the ones that are self-sufficient to go out and live in the community but I think the administration's ideas are a little unreal. We have had several cases where they go out, and have walked right back in. Remember there have already been a lot of changes and the better higher grade residents are gone now, so the ones that are left are . . . well, it's just touch and go whether they can make it or not. They might stay out for a while and then they're back in. Most of those that could make it are out and have stayed there, so you get a circulation of those that go out and come back every couple of months.

There are other things that influence their behaviour outside. Often the psychiatrists that look after them start playing around with their medications and it puts their whole behaviour pattern out of whack. I'm not talking about the people themselves forgetting their medications or fooling around with them. I'm talking about the doctor's orders being changed. We had a girl who's my resident. She can be very aggressive and uncooperative and we got her to a point where she could go do work on a short program on the ward and her behaviour was fine. Well, she'd been good for so long that the doctor thought that maybe he could cut her medication. It had been tried before and it had always been the same. So he cut it and it was only a week after that she tried to bite the girl that was working with her. Now we're back where we were in the first place.

We're their surrogate parents, that's what we are. We do a little bit of everything. We feed them, wash them, dress them—the ones that need that kind of help. We give a bit of treatment. We do medications. We teach them self-help skills. Adults with the mental grade they're at, are easy to take care of if you have the right attitude. You develop a kind of off-the-cuff attitude. We'd be joking with them, or laughing with them or at them, or whatever you like—and to them, well, they like that. But if you would come and stand back looking, you'd think we were terrible people. One way of getting some residents motivated is to tease them. It's not the way they write in the books as the way to do it, but it works. And if it's the only thing that works, then you use it. Some of the residents thrive on being teased because that's their attention. They enjoy it. You have 28 or 30 residents, and you have to be flexible. Different things can make them do things, and you have to adapt to how they react.

KEEPER
Maximum Security Prison

Comments

He has managed to maintain contact with the prisoners in an environment which systematically discourages it. He counts former convicts among his friends. He tells me about the trouble he's had in keeping an older alcoholic inmate out of the clutches of his parole officer, "sobering him up every night so that he could get to work in the morning. Now he is off the liquor. He's married and is beginning to get on—he has a bit of a heart condition. We see each other around. It still makes me feel good that he made it out of here."

When he leaves the office after the interview, I find that I have run out of cigarettes and I want a coffee before the next one. The only other person around is an inmate-cleaner. He says the canteen isn't open and there is no coffee machine. So I return to the office to wait for the next interviewee. Soon he comes in with a mug of coffee and a handful of cigarettes, "Because I saw that you were talking to Mr. Rathwell and I'm giving these to you to show you how much I think of him."

Mr. Rathwell is a distinguished and somewhat military-looking man of 60. He has a quiet calm manner. He treats all convicts as prisoners of war. They are in prison through no fault of their own, should be free of the system once they are released, and have the right to plan and execute escapes so long as they do not harm anyone. He has no fear of contamination by them and he intersperses his stories with a history of the gradual change in the prison to allow for more contact with prisoners.

How much is our attitude to institutions related to a fear that we might end up in one of them through no fault of our own? To be innocent in prison, sane in a mental hospital, lucid in a long-stay hospital is a modern nightmare. This keeper recognizes that all inmates feel unjustly incarcerated. They are like prisoners of war who feel that they have come to the Stalag through no fault of their own.

This keeper is in many ways unique. He is the only keeper in this book with the job title "keeper," yet he seems the least stereotypical of the keepers. He goes against our preconceptions of institutions and those who work in them. He has a special capacity to maintain a difficult perspective in the face of a contradictory institutional culture. It is useful to see that not everyone associated with harmful institutions must be harmed by them and that it is possible to find means of personal survival which do not depend on conformity or collusion with the institutional system. This can help us realize how much we all distance ourselves not only from the institutions but also from the keepers.

Interview

I am the Senior Keeper. There are eight keepers here and I am a supervising keeper or Chief Keeper which is overall staff assistant to the Deputy Governor in charge of Security.

I started here after the army. I came here as Guard Grade 1. I moved on to Guard Grade 2 and later became a Keeper before I was promoted to Chief Keeper. At the time I started, there were a lot of people out of the service that came to work here. Today, there's a lot of people who started back around the time I did and they're retiring, so usually the opportunity of moving up today is faster than it was then. There's only one other staff member who started before I did. He started a month before I did. The rest are all later than that.

When I came here, you didn't have the contact with the inmates that you do today. You had contact with them but not verbally. You were instructed to talk to them very little. Your job was to put them in the cell and lock the cell. And the Grade 1 Guard, as it was at that time, had little to do with them other than telling them to get in their cells and where to go and so on, but they never came to you with any requests or complaints as they do today. At that time, their exercise in the yard consisted of walking around in a circle in silence. When they moved through the yard to and from work, it was in silence. They didn't talk to each other. They kept in single file and they were locked in their cells about 4:00 in the afternoon until 7:30 the next morning when they started eating breakfast. At night, they had radio programs to listen to but they consisted of large speakers and all the programs were monitored, and news flashes that had to do with prisons were cut out before they came on. They didn't have any newspapers and after 8:00 at night, a bell rang for silence, supposedly to give inmates who wanted to study a chance for that. There was no talking after 8:00 at night and they never came out of their cells till the next morning. There were no sports or anything like that.

Later, they started the hobby system which gave inmates some diversion—something to work at in their cells in the evening and they started having ball games, boxing matches, different sports in the yard. They got an inmate canteen in the yard and I don't think there was anything like it in any other prison. They could go out in the yard, they could buy coffee, cold drinks, hot dogs, stuff like this. They wrecked the thing in a riot and that was the finish of the canteen in the yard.

At one time, we had up to 1100 in here at once. That's an approximate figure. Sometimes it went above and sometimes it went below but the female prison was included on our calendar. The main cellblock here held 614 inmates. It was pretty well filled all the time. There are 614 cells, or were at that time, but pretty well the whole cellblock was sabotaged and wrecked in a riot and only a portion of it was renovated, so we have a lot of it not in use now and we don't have nearly that many cells now. There was talk that they were going to renovate it.

This building that we are in, years ago long before my time, was a female prison. There was a wall around here. When I came here, it was called the Old Man's Home or Northwest Cellblock. There were old inmates who were doing life or long sentences. They had a lot of time in and it was the only area in the institution where inmates were allowed to get outside on the landings here and play cards at night. There were two floors of it. It was mostly older inmates who had served a lot of time.

Then we had another cellblock, the East Cellblock, the two bottom floors were used for segregation for disciplinary problems and some who couldn't get along with other inmates. There was just a few locked up there—psychiatric cases before they were moved to hospitals. The two upper floors were larger cells than the main cellblock and were reserved for better behaved inmates and ones doing a long time. They were given a chance to move into these cells which were much larger and it was a privilege for an inmate to be in there. The East Cellblock held 114 inmates and it was later converted to include a psychiatric centre.

You probably wondered when I said there was over 1100 where we housed them all. At one time, we had six dormitories in here which held about 45 inmates apiece so that was where the overflow from the cellblocks went. Some inmates liked sleeping in the dormitories, others didn't. They wanted their privacy and preferred to be in a cell but there are no dormitories here now. At one time there were the six dormitories.

It was and still is classified as maximum security as you can see by the walls and the towers. There have been changes. They brought in a system where inmates for compassionate reasons, like a death in the family, they could be escorted to the funerals, or if someone was seriously ill. That was one of the changes that took place where it had been unheard of before. I think at the time there was so much came in so fast that even the inmates found it hard to handle, and in a lot of institutions discipline was very lax. Even a lot of inmates didn't like this because they felt that they were safer in an institution where there was more discipline, and of course, a lot of them had got used to being told what to do and what they couldn't do. Some of them rebelled at the time but by the same token, a lot of them liked it the old way because they were institutionalized.

On the other hand, not everything had changed. One time an inmate wrote to me after he went out and said he had got a job and wouldn't be back. They put it down as a mark against me. I was called up in front of the board saying I had a letter from an ex-inmate. They said, "This was wrong, you are not supposed to communicate." This is another way it's changed. Anybody who wants to become involved here and try and help an inmate can do more than they could then. I've had phone calls from inmates and letters from all over the country. There's one inmate who has been out for 10 years and every Christmas, he phones me long distance to tell me he is getting along all right, and it's not frowned upon the way it was in those days. The guard who feels so inclined can talk to an inmate and counsel him about staying out; there is a better way than spending time in here. It's not frowned upon.

For me, it has made my work better. Of course I don't think like every member of the staff. Some of the staff find it hard to deal with them with no numbers on them, identifying them and so on. Some of the staff feel they have a little too much freedom to what they used to have.

I like my job here. I enjoy dealing with inmates and I feel I can deal with them effectively. I have been told by one person who was assistant deputy governor here at the time, "You have the ability to be tough if need be, and still be humane and go the other way if you have to."

The relationship in this institution between the treatment staff and the security staff, I think surpasses the relationship in any other institution I've been to, and I've been to a lot of them. There is a good relationship between the two and my feeling is we are all in the same business and we work together, and I think we do work together very well here. I think it is to all our benefits to work together and I find out things from them to help me and vice versa.

Certainly, there are times when there is a conflict between us. I may know something they don't know. That's why I sit on these boards like the Inmate Treatment Board. I may be able to tell them something they don't know about the person and that has a bearing on how the case is dealt with, and I think it's only right that it should be that way. They do the same for me. They tell me things I don't know about the man and it may have a bearing on my dealing with him.

At times, they may have an inmate up for an interview and he puts his best foot forward trying to impress them to get what he wants, and they have no idea how he behaves down in the cellblock or in the shop or wherever. I am around there and I see what goes on and know that while he may not get himself in serious trouble, so that he is locked up or anything like that, his whole attitude in general isn't very good. And he could come up here and try to put on a different front altogether. I think the inmates realize that there is a different relationship here now between security or correctional staff and the treatment staff, and there isn't so much of them coming up and trying to impress the treatment staff with something or being something that they are really not.

At the same time, you can get a correctional officer who feels the only way is to lock them up and throw the key away. I might feel that it's not in our best interests or in the inmates' best interests to take that route so we try and deal with whatever problem he was having in some other way. The staff may resent it a little if I deal with it some other way instead of locking the man up. I do try and explain to them why. I try and impress upon them that there is a better way if you can deal with him.

Now, there are times you run across the type of inmate that the only recourse is to lock him up to show him who's the boss because we do run across out-and-out rebels who just don't want to conform in any way. But by and large, I don't have too much conflict with staff, although some of them may resent what I do a little. They say, "Well, if it was me who was doing that, I would throw him in the hole and leave him," which I don't agree with. I feel that in here, it's the same as a policeman's job in the street, to prevent crime rather than let it go and be committed. It's part of my job, I feel, to keep an inmate out of trouble rather than getting in. So if I can talk to him, I try and solve the problem some other way.

Sometimes it takes talking to both staff and inmates to convince them that change is perhaps for all our benefits, and that it will work and can work if both groups contribute to it. And a lot of time if you can explain the reason for it to them, you will get the cooperation and I think it helps to make it work—whatever the change may be.

Mind you, I think they have gone a little overboard with prisoners' rights. When I came here, I remembered the Governor seeing every new inmate that came in. At that time, he said, "The rights you have here are the rights to three meals a day, a bed to sleep in, clothing and medical care." But it has progressed far beyond that. The people outside who are screaming about prisoners' rights, I often think why don't they waste time or spend some time on the rights of the victims. If they want to do some good, there has certainly got to be an area there where they can do some good. I think they have gone overboard on prisoners' rights.

Everything has a grievance procedure now. I think there are grounds for grievance procedures but it extends to petty things. They have the accident report if something happens to either staff or inmate and I have no quarrel with that. It should be to protect the staff, inmates and the institution.

That's another thing we are talking about—searching an inmate. God help us if it ever comes to where we can't search them. I think that more inmates' lives would probably be in danger. Over the past few years, violence has increased in various places. We have been fortunate here because we pretty much can tell what's going on, but if we couldn't search a man, he could be trying anything. It wouldn't be very good.

Staff is watched here all the time. I was told by an inmate one time I caught with illegal pills on him and money on him. He said, "You never should have caught me. You have been under the watch here. We can spend our time watching you or anybody else who might be a threat to us, or who might get wise to what we're doing." He said, "I was wise that you knew something was going on this morning." I said, "How did you know?" And he said, "Well, you came in the recreation building, and all the inmates were in there." And he said, "Normally you move around and talk to several inmates and several of the staff but this morning you came in and you talked to one staff member." Which I did do and I had told him, "Don't let that man leave this building without taking him and searching him." And he was observant enough that he knew by my moves that morning, he said, "So right then I knew that you were wise that there was something going on."

You watch them, well that's very true but they figure, "I can spend as much time watching him as he can watching me." You get used to being watched. You get to feel the mood of the place when something is about to happen. It might just be their reaction if I walk into a place like a gym and it all goes quiet. Nobody comes to talk to you. There's something going on.

I think that long-term institutionalization has a terrible impact on a man. The classic example appeared two weeks ago on Friday. I flew with an inmate to the city to put him on a plane to send him home. He had come into the institution when he was 17 and he was going out after 11 years and he had been heavily involved in a riot here. He had been in institutions all across the country and had been transferred all over the place and back here into the psychiatric unit, and he was going out after 11 years and he was absolutely terrified. He was afraid I was going to leave him before he would get on the plane.

We flew from here in a small five- or six-seater plane to the city. He was afraid that the plane might not be safe. While he had been flown to other places during the time he was incarcerated, he was absolutely terrified of getting on a plane by himself. He was all right as long as I was with him. Of course he had known me all the time he was doing time.

After we arrived in the city, he said, "You won't leave me before I get on the plane, will you?" And he said, "Will I have to sit with other people?" While he had some contact with ministers, etc., within the institution, that was his home ground but he is going onto a plane where they are all free people and he was terrified of perhaps sitting next to someone he didn't know.

When we arrived at the gate where he was to go down to board the plane, they told me I couldn't go down to the plane and he became terrified. I don't know whether he would have gone through the gate. I got the airport security to take me right through to the plane and we got on it together.

I understand he got in trouble that weekend and they caught him a short time after going out. But he was really paranoid—he was so paranoid that the stewardesses on the plane knew that he was nervous when we got on and they were aware of where he came from, and they were going to try and help him out during the flight but it had a terrible impact on him—being turned loose after that length of time.

Others who perhaps have abided by the rules and got along and have had the occasional pass out during the time of their incarceration, are not quite the same. Of course, it's the make-up of the man quite a lot too how it affects him when he is going out. I have taken others on pass who have been in some length of time and it doesn't seem to bother them so much at all. I don't believe he would have got on the plane had he not been taken to it. I have seen people come back after a very, very short time out.

This particular fellow I took to the city, he wanted to buy cigarettes before he got on the plane and he was shocked. He was used to buying them in here at a cheap price and he was shocked at the prices now. He had no idea or concept of the difference of price in things. Although his family were to meet him, when he did eventually get off that plane, it was quite a shock to the system. The same as coming inside these gates for the man who has never been in jail before. I've told inmates myself, "I went through the same thing when I arrived; I wondered what the hell I had got myself into so I can appreciate how you feel the first time you come in." The gates close behind him and he's inside these walls.

I remember quite clearly thinking to myself the first time I walked in, "Why did I ever come here?" Of course at that time, like a lot of people, we were just arriving from overseas. I was married, had a child and I thought well, there weren't that many jobs around. I wanted to be able to support my family and so on, and I'd never been in any kind of setting like this. You had to find out a lot for yourself then. They didn't have the staff training they have today so you weren't prepared in any way for it.

Now my day is pretty well-structured. I'm here at 7:00 in the morning and I arrange for guards to escort inmates to outside hospitals, to court, and transfers out of the institution to other institutions. The rest of my time is comprised in sitting on various boards: Initial Placement Board which is selecting the institution that inmates will be transferred to; Inmate Training Board where they recommend inmates for transfers or open visits out of the institution; Inmate Work Boards for selecting inmates for various jobs in the institution. It's a pretty busy day and I do spend a lot of time with inmates who request to see me. Most of them know me, especially the repeaters. I make a trip all around the various posts within the institution where staff are in the shops. I usually do that twice a day—morning and afternoon, so I have a pretty full day. There's 11 acres inside the wall here.

I don't give being a keeper of other men a lot of thought any more other than it's part of my job. I remember being duty officer and going over to a hospital in town. Just before I arrived there an inmate had tried to escape. They caught him at the door trying to leave. He had pushed the wrong door and it led to a locked double door. A staff member took him back up. When I arrived there, they told me he tried to escape so I'm bringing him back. I arranged for a car to take him over. He said, "You're not angry with me?" And I said, "No, why should I be?" He said, "I just tried to escape." I said, "So what. I stopped you and it's part of the game. It's our job to keep you here, and I don't know that if I were in your shoes I wouldn't try the same thing."

I have worked in this institution for going on 30 years now and especially now with a man that's sentenced to 25 years before parole, I can visualize myself if I were in that situation. I would think, "That's forever," and I think it would be perfectly normal to try to escape. Certainly it's our job as correctional officers to stop the escape, but I can't see how anyone can blame the man for trying. I wouldn't look kindly on someone getting smashed over the head or killed in an escape attempt. I went to Mexico with a prisoner exchange and met a person at the embassy that had a lot to do with prisons down there. He told me that in Mexico they believe that the prisoner has the right to try to escape. Quite often, if a prisoner does escape, the Governor takes his place in the prison.

www.ingramcontent.com/pod-product-compliance
Lightning Source LLC
Chambersburg PA
CBHW030254030426
42336CB00009B/382